THE MARGARET THATCHER BOOK OF QUOTATIONS

THE MARGARET THATCHER BOOK OF QUOTATIONS

EDITED BY IAIN DALE AND GRANT TUCKER

Biteback Publishing

First published in Great Britain in 2012 by
Biteback Publishing Ltd
Westminster Tower
3 Albert Embankment
London SE1 7SP
Selection and editorial apparatus copyright © Iain Dale and Grant Tucker 2012

ISBN 978-1-84954-383-5

10 9 8 7 6 5 4 3 2 1

A CIP catalogue record for this book is available from the British Library.

Set in Chronicle and Grotesque

Printed and bound in Great Britain by
CPI Group (UK) Ltd, Croydon CR0 4YY

CONTENTS

FOREWORD

It was a cold evening in February. The boy was only twelve years old, yet he knew that something historic had just happened. He tiptoed up the stairs to the bedroom, where his eighty-year-old grandmother lay in bed, suffering from flu. Having gauged that she was indeed awake, he approached the bed.

The woman who lay there was a formidable personality in her own right. She dominated her family in a matriarchal style, reminiscent of the woman who that day had won the leadership of the Conservative Party.

'She's won,' he said. Silence. 'No, really, she's won,' he protested. Slowly, a tear ran down her face. 'It's not possible,' she murmured. 'It's just not possible.'

That boy was me. Even at such a young age I was interested in politics. I wasn't a Conservative. Only six months earlier, I remember walking into my parents' bedroom with my own thoughts on who should win the general election. I read it to my parents, who quite obviously had a good night's sleep higher on their priority list. 'All the Conservatives ever did was take us into Europe,'

I exclaimed. 'The Liberals have no chance of winning,' I said, with a remarkable degree of accuracy. 'So, give Labour a chance,' I advised. 'Don't be so stupid,' said my father. 'Go back to bed.'

My early teenage years were spent supporting David Steel's Liberals. My parents had both voted Liberal in 1974, more as a protest against Edward Heath than anything, but my mother said she would not be able to vote for them again after Jeremy Thorpe had disgraced himself.

Like most of my school friends and teachers I found it easy to poke fun at Mrs Thatcher. It was certainly not fashionable to be a Conservative in the mid-1970s. But one day, in October 1978, I heard her speech to the Tory Party Conference. I remember thinking at the end of it that I agreed with virtually everything she said. I got hold of a few policy documents and at the age of sixteen I joined the local Conservative Party.

My first tentative footstep into the political arena was to set up a Conservative organisation in 1982 at the very left-wing University of East Anglia. Only a few months later followed my first encounter with Margaret Thatcher when she invited the chairmen of the various university Conservative Associations to a reception at No. 10.

For a country boy like me, it was unbelievable to have been invited and it was something I had been looking forward to for months. Just to climb those stairs with the portraits of all past Prime Ministers on the wall was worth the trip on its own. And there at the top of the stairs was the Prime Minister. She had obviously perfected the art of welcoming people to receptions and as she shook you by the hand and wished you a good evening, she moved you on into the room without you even knowing she was doing it. Most of the Cabinet were there – I remember discussing with Cecil Parkinson the number of free running shoes he had been sent after a recent profile had announced to the world that he was a keen runner. He offered me a pair but it turned out his feet were much smaller than mine! We were constantly plied with wine and I made a mental note to stop at two glasses. But after the second glass was emptied I felt rather self-conscious without a glass in my hand so grabbed another. Just as the Prime Minister walked by I took a sip. All I remember is my stomach heaving and me thinking that I was about to throw up at the Prime Minister's feet, thus ending a glorious political career which had hardly got off the ground. Luckily I managed to control my stomach and all was well. It turned out that it was whisky in my glass, rather than white wine.

Later in the evening, as I was talking to my local MP, Alan Haselhurst, the division bell sounded. Although there were at least forty MPs there, none made a move to leave to go and vote over the road in the House of Commons. Mrs Thatcher started to look rather irritated and was obviously none too impressed. In the end she walked to the middle of the room, took off one of her shoes and banged it on the floor. There was instant silence. The Prime Minister then spoke. 'Would all Conservative MPs kindly leave the building immediately,' she instructed. 'And the rest of us will stay and enjoy ourselves!'

Naturally we all laughed uproariously, enjoying the sight of the MPs trooping out of the room in a somewhat sheepish manner.

After I graduated I went to work at the House of Commons as a researcher for a Norfolk Member of Parliament. He was not a particularly well-known MP and never courted publicity. He had a marginal seat and devoted himself to his constituency rather than join the rent-a-quote mob. It served him well as he held his seat for the next two elections. If ever there was an MP less likely to be involved in sleaze it was him. But one day, a careless error by me left him open to charges of dirty dealing. We ran a businessman's club in the constituency, called The Westminster Circle. It served two purposes – first, to keep the MP in touch with local businesses, and second, to raise a little more money for the very poor constituency association. For £100 a year business people joined and were given a dinner in the House of Commons, usually addressed by a Cabinet minister, and another dinner in the constituency, addressed by a more junior minister. These clubs were common in all parties up and down the country. But in a publicity leaflet designed to attract new members I used the phrase 'with direct access to Government minister'. By this I had meant they would be able to meet and speak to a Government minister at the dinner. In those pre 'cash for questions' days we were all rather innocent. But it proved to be my undoing – and very nearly my employer's.

Early one Tuesday afternoon he found out that at that day's Prime Minister's Question Time, the Liberal leader,

David Steel, would raise this subject with the Prime Minister. He immediately went to see her in her office behind the Speaker's Chair. He must have been quaking in his boots but he later told me she had been brilliant. She sat him down, offered him a coffee and heard him out. She did not disguise her dislike for Steel and thought it was typical of him to operate in this manner. She told him she would let Steel have both barrels, and of course she did! He returned to the office after PM's Question Time and related the events of the day to me. I had been completely oblivious, which was just as well as I would no doubt have been having a premonition of what a P45 looked like.

A few months later I was having lunch with a couple of Tory MPs in the Members' Cafeteria. We had just finished our lunch when in walked Mrs T. and her entourage. She grabbed a tray and chose a light lunch of Welsh rarebit. Unfortunately, as we had finished, I did not have cause to hang around too much longer so left the room, cursing that we had decided to have an early lunch. A few minutes later I realised I had left some papers and magazines on the table in the cafeteria and returned to retrieve them. As luck would have it, the Thatcher group had sat themselves at the table we had been sitting at and Mrs T. had her elbow plonked on my papers. I decided to summon up the courage and interrupt them to ask for my papers. Just as I had started I looked down at the pile of papers and to my horror saw that my copy of the new issue of *Private Eye* was on the top of them and with a front cover of a particularly nasty photo of Denis Thatcher. Mrs Thatcher cottoned on to what I wanted, removed her elbow, and gazed down at the offending magazine. My heart stopped. 'Oh, *Private Eye*, Denis loves it,' she gushed. To my eternal shame, I just picked it up, along with the rest of my papers, made my excuses and left. What a wimp.

In 1994 I took an American friend, Daniel Forrester, to the T. E. Utley Young Journalist of the Year awards at the Reform Club. Lady Thatcher had been invited to present the awards. She treated us to a half-hour impromptu speech on political issues of the moment, which seemed to go by in about five minutes – quite an achievement as her entire audience had to remain standing throughout. After she had finished, Daniel whispered to me: 'I have to meet her, what should I do?' Knowing her penchant for strapping, six feet tall, dark-haired American men I encouraged him to go and introduce himself. He suddenly got cold feet so eventually I dragged him over to where she was talking to several of the award winners. In typically American style he launched into a sycophantic introduction which immediately attracted her attention. 'Mrs Thatcher,' he began. I kicked him. 'Er, Lady Thatcher,' he hurriedly corrected himself, 'May I say how much our country misses your leadership...' and he continued in that vein for a few seconds. While he was speaking, the diminutive figure of the Iron Lady (for she is much smaller in height than most people imagine) stared up at him, her eyes never leaving his. When he had finally finished having his say, Lady Thatcher hardly paused or breathed. 'Your President, President Clinton.' She paused, heightening the drama for my American friend. 'He is a great communicator.' Up came the forefinger, almost prodding Daniel's chest. Then in a particularly contemptuous tone, came the pièce de résistance: 'The trouble is, he has absolutely nothing to communicate.' With that she was away. It was almost a flounce. Daniel eventually came down from whichever cloud he had been on – probably nine – and said, 'I'll remember that for the rest of my life' – and, as a well-known critic of Bill Clinton, has been dining out on it ever since.

Another encounter came at a retirement party for ITN's much-missed political editor Michael Brunson. My friend Alan Duncan, the Tory MP for Rutland, started a conversation with her and she suddenly asked where Denis had disappeared off to as they had to leave for dinner. Being of diminutive stature, and me being over six feet tall, she asked me to scan the room. Both of them looked at me expectantly. To my horror I spied Denis on the other side of the room talking to Michael Heseltine. I summoned up all the courage at my disposal and explained where he was. Lady Thatcher's eyes became even bluer than normal and she exclaimed: 'Denis and I are having dinner with Cap Weinberger tonight. I think he's rather more important than THAT man, don't you?! If Denis isn't over here within one minute I shall go over and stare at them.' Luckily for Michael Heseltine, she didn't have to.

Early in 2005 I invited Lady Thatcher to come to a fundraising party to raise money for my campaign as Conservative candidate for North Norfolk. To my delight she accepted and on a cold March evening turned up on time to work a room of fifty friends and political acquaintances. And boy did she work! She was particularly pleased to meet the teenagers present, including one with a particularly eye-catching piece of metal face jewellery. My task for the evening was to guide Lady T. around the room so she could meet everyone. It was a thankless task. The Iron Lady decided where she was going and no amount of me tugging at her elbow was going to persuade her otherwise!

And then, in November 2005 I launched my book, *Margaret Thatcher: A Tribute in Words & Pictures,* at a function in the City of London, kindly hosted by the Corporation of London. Lady Thatcher agreed to attend and made a point of speaking to everyone in the room while she was there. Especially poignant for me was the sight of her having a protracted chat with my two nieces, Isabella and Ophelia Hunter, who were then aged ten and six. It was a very touching moment as they posed for pictures. It brought back a memory from 1988, when my cousin Nicola's daughter Emma – then an infant – asked her mother: 'Mummy, can a man be Prime Minister?' She soon found out that the answer was no.

The last time I spoke to Lady Thatcher was in January 2009 when I went to the Carlton Club for a drinks party hosted by Liam Fox. I was delighted to see Lady Thatcher arrive and looking absolutely fantastic. For a woman of eighty-three and supposedly in frail health, she looked absolutely stunning.

I had a couple of minutes talking to her and told her it was twenty-six years to the day that I first met her at a reception for Conservative students at 10 Downing

Street. 'I think I remember that,' she said. 'It was so nice to see so many young people in the building. That didn't happen very often.' We talked a little about newspapers and she said: 'I never read them. I had Bernard to do it for me.' Everyone needs a Bernard...

As I left the Carlton Club, a thought struck me. If Lady T. were in her heyday and had to take over as Prime Minister now, what would she do? If I had asked her, I know exactly what her reply would have been. 'Restore sound money, dear,' she would have said. And you know what? She'd have been dead right.

The lady inspired and maintained my interest in politics. I think that can be said for many of my generation. She inspired admiration and hate in equal quantities. Rarely has a British politician ever been so loved and reviled at the same time. Few have been satirised to the degree she was.

But she had her failings too, something even her greatest admirers will readily admit. She was not a particularly good judge of character and made some appalling ministerial appointments, which in the end contributed greatly to her downfall. She was not a good listener, something many a world leader will testify to. But having said that, she loved a good argument. It is said that John Major first came to her notice when he stood up to her and argued his case.

Her achievements outweigh any of her failings. She restored this country's faith in itself, rescued our industry from the shackles of trade union domination and cured the economy of inflation. She fought for freedom and challenged dictators. She played a pivotal role in bringing about the end of Communism, standing firm by the side of President Reagan. She was the first to see that Mikhail Gorbachev was a different kind of Soviet leader. For all this she will be remembered as a dominant force in the final quarter of the twentieth century. Was she one of our great Prime Ministers, joining the ranks of Lloyd George, Churchill, Gladstone, Disraeli and Attlee? History will be the judge.

This book is meant to give the reader both an insight into the character of Margaret Thatcher and her political views, and an historical record of the Thatcher years in her own words and the words of those who were there with her. No collection of quotes can ever be all-encompassing, and this one certainly does not pretend to be. What it does, is show how her personality developed from childhood into the powerful, self-confident politician who achieved the highest office in the land. It includes quotes from her opponents as well as her allies. As the editor, I make no secret of my admiration for Margaret Thatcher and her achievements, but this book is not a hagiography of quotations. It is, instead, an accessible record of the Thatcher years of power.

I would like to thank friends and colleagues who have given frank and helpful advice during the preparation of this book and been of great support to me. In addition, I would like to thank the staff of Westminster Reference Library for their kindness and help.

I am grateful to Sir Bernard Ingham for allowing me to reproduce the *Yes, Prime Minister* sketch. Parliamentary copyright material from Hansard is reproduced with the permission of Her Majesty's Stationery Office on behalf of Parliament.

I have listed many of the sources for this book in a bibliography at the end as they are too numerous to mention here. Where possible I have provided the original source for the individual quotes. I have also added a contextual explanation where I thought it necessary. Any errors are mine alone. And Grant Tucker's, of course!

Finally, I would like to thank Lady Thatcher herself – it can never be more true to say that this book would not have been possible without her.

Iain Dale
Norfolk, July 2012

EARLY YEARS

I wasn't lucky – I deserved it.

Receiving a prize for poetry, aged nine

◆

I owe a great deal to the church for everything in which I believe. I am very glad that I was brought up strictly... I was a very serious child... There was not a lot of fun and sparkle in my life.

Daily Telegraph, June 1980

◆

I was brought up by a Victorian grandmother. We were taught to work jolly hard. We were taught to prove yourself; we were taught self-reliance; we were taught to live within our income. You were taught that cleanliness is next to godliness. You were taught self respect. You were taught always to give a hand to your neighbour. You were taught tremendous pride in your country. All of these things are Victorian values. They are also perennial values. You don't hear so much about these things these days, but they were good values and they led to tremendous improvements in the standard of living.

LBC Radio, April 1983

◆

She was a perfectly good second-class chemist. None of us ever thought that she would go very far. One could always rely on her to produce a sensible, well-read essay and yet there was something that some people had that she hadn't quite got. I don't believe she had a particularly profound interest in chemistry.

Dorothy Hodgkin, Margaret Thatcher's tutor at Oxford

◆

I went to Oxford University, but I've never let that hold me back.

Conservative Party Conference, 13 October 1989

◆

This woman is headstrong, obstinate and dangerously self-opinionated.

Report on Margaret Roberts by the ICI Personnel Department, rejecting her job application, 1948

◆

When hecklers stand up ... I get a mental jump for joy. It gives me something to get my teeth into – and the audiences love it.

Daily Graphic, 1951

◆

For some time now I have been fleeing the temptation to return to active politics. I had intended, when I was called to the Bar, to concentrate entirely on legal work but a little experience at the Revenue Bar, and in company matters, far from turning my attention from politics, has served to draw my attention more closely to the body which is responsible for the legislation about which I have come to hold strong views.

Letter to Donald Kaberry, Vice Chairman of the Conservative Party, written in February 1956. *The Path to Power*, 1995

◆

I suppose I was about twenty, and a crowd of us had been to a village hop and came back to make midnight cups of coffee. I was in the kitchen helping to dish up and having a fierce argument with one of the boys in the crowd when someone else interrupted to say: 'Of course Margaret, you will go into politics won't you?' I stopped dead. Suddenly it was crystallised for me. I knew.

Daily Express, April 1961

◆

I had the most marvellous upbringing; it stayed with me the rest of my life. It was, I always thought, a very tough upbringing. I was taught from my early years at school, taught by my father, to make up my own mind about my views, to say, 'This is what I believe in, this is what I am going to do.' Then you perhaps find that maybe the crowd comes with you. But never go with the crowd for the sake of going with the crowd – never, never, never. My goodness, it was hard as a young person; it was hard, but it was right.

Sunday Telegraph, 14 February 1982

◆

When I was young I was taught at home this little doggerel:
    It's easy to be a starter,
    But are you a sticker too?
    It's easy enough to begin a job,
    It's harder to see it through.

Reader's Digest, January 1984

◆

I loved my mother dearly, but after I was fifteen we had nothing more to say to each other. It wasn't her fault. She was weighed down by the home, always being in the home.

Daily Express, April 1961

◆

One of my favourite quotations is: 'That which thy father bequeathed thee, earn it anew, if thou wouldst possess it.'

◆

It is expensive to be in politics. One has to be mobile, one has to be well groomed, and one has to entertain.

The Guardian, March 1962

◆

We must recognise certain groups of people who need help, but the rest of us must take responsibility for ourselves, and we must stop being such a subsidised-minded society.

Scottish Conservative Party Conference, May 1969

◆

This business of the working class is on its way out I think. After all, aren't I working class? I work jolly hard, I can tell you.

London Evening News, October 1969

◆

I speak as a very young Tory, and we are entitled to speak for it is the people of my generation who will bear the brunt of the change from the trials of the past into calmer channels.

Speech in Sleaford, 29 June 1945

◆

Comprehensive schools will have gone out in ten or fifteen years' time.

1970

◆

I've no idea why people keep attacking me. I don't deserve it at all.

Sunday Express, 16 January 1972

◆

I'm not hard, I'm frightfully soft – but I will not be hounded. I will not be driven anywhere against my will.

Daily Mail, 1972

◆

Please don't use the word tough. People might get the impression that I don't care. And I do care very deeply. Resilient, I think.

August 1973

◆

I enjoyed my early Ministerial career: it was an absorbing education both in the ways of Whitehall and in the technicalities of pensions policy. But I could not help noticing a curious discrepancy in the behaviour of my colleagues. What they said and what they did seemed to exist in two separate compartments. It was not that they conspicuously deceived anyone; they were in fact conspicuously honourable. But the language of free enterprise, anti-Socialism and the national interest sprang readily to their lips, while they conducted Government business on very different assumptions about the role of the state at home and of the nation state abroad.

The Downing Street Years, 1993

◆

I don't want to be leader of the party – I'm happy to be in the top dozen.

1974

◆

We failed the people.

On the Heath Government, *Daily Telegraph*, February 1974

◆

It was then that the iron entered my soul.

On the Heath Government

◆

We went back on a very similar manifesto to things I believe in. The difference is that after eighteen months to two years he did the biggest U-turn on policy of all time and started to go the wrong way. In the end, that cost us the next election.

On the Heath Government, 18 June 1990

◆

The charm of Britain has always been the ease with which one can move into the middle class.

London Evening Standard, October 1974

◆

Look Keith, if you're not going to stand, I will.

To Sir Keith Joseph after he decided not to stand against Edward Heath for the party leadership

◆

Forget that I'm a woman. Forget the accusation that I am a right-winger demanding privilege – I had precious little privilege in my early years.

February 1975

◆

I've got my teeth into him, and I'm not going to let go.

On Edward Heath during the leadership contest, February 1975

◆

Now we have lots of work to do.

To Norman St John-Stevas, who broke the news to her that she
had won the first round of the leadership contest, February 1975

◆

To me it is like a dream that the next name in the list after
Harold Macmillan, Sir Alec Douglas-Home and Edward
Heath is Margaret Thatcher.

February 1975

◆

I always cheer up immensely if an attack is particularly
wounding because I think, well, if they attack me personally it means they have not a single political argument left.

◆

The better I do, the more is expected of me. I am ready for
that. I think I have the strength to do anything that I feel
has to be done.

Daily Telegraph, September 1975

◆

I confess that I am quite pleased that I didn't continue
my work on glyceride monolayers in the early 1950s or I
might never have got here at all!

On her previous career as a chemist, 27 September 1988

ON THATCHERISM

You cannot bring about prosperity by discouraging thrift.

You cannot strengthen the weak by weakening the strong.

You cannot help the wage earner by pulling down the wage payer.

You cannot further the brotherhood by encouraging class hatred.

You cannot help the poor by destroying the rich.

You cannot establish sound security on borrowed money.

You cannot keep out of trouble by spending more than you earn.

You cannot build character and courage by taking away man's initiative and independence.

You cannot help men permanently by doing for them what they could and should do for themselves.

Abraham Lincoln, kept by Mrs Thatcher in her handbag

◆

We should back the workers, not the shirkers.

February 1974

◆

We must have an ideology. The other side have got an ideology they can test their policies against. We must have one as well.

1975

◆

The path that we now take is the path that the people have chosen.

1979

◆

Let our children grow tall, and some grow taller than others.

Speech in the United States, 1975

◆

We must build a society in which each citizen can develop his full potential, both for his benefit and for the community as a whole.

1975

◆

The next Conservative Government will look forward to discussion and consultation with the trade union movement about the policies that are now needed to save our country.

Conservative Party Conference, Brighton, October 1976

♦

If your only opportunity is to be equal then it is not opportunity.

28 November 1976

♦

Britain is no longer in the politics of the pendulum, but of the ratchet.

1977

♦

We want a society in which we are free to make choices, to make mistakes, to be generous and compassionate. That is what we mean by a moral society – not a society in which the state is responsible for everything, and no one is responsible for the state.

At Zurich University, 14 March 1977

♦

Sometimes I've heard it said that Conservatives have been associated with unemployment. That's absolutely wrong. We'd have been drummed out of office if we'd had this level of unemployment.

Party political broadcast, May 1977, when unemployment was 1.3 million

◆

If the unions hold the whip hand, upon whose back does the lash fall?

25 September 1977

◆

I, personally, have always voted for the death penalty because I believe that people who go out prepared to take the lives of other people forfeit their own right to live. I believe that the death penalty should be used only very rarely, but I believe that no one should go out certain that no matter how cruel, how vicious, how hideous their murder, they themselves will not suffer the death penalty.

◆

Defeat? I do not recognise the meaning of the word.

◆

Class is a Communist concept. It groups people as bundles and sets them against one another. I remember practically exploding when I heard some Americans talking about 'the underclass,' as if they weren't individuals with feelings. Each one is entitled to his own dignity, to develop his talents and abilities. Underclass? Socialist claptrap! That's why I began by talking about liberty. The more you talk about class – or even about 'classlessness' – the more you fix the idea in people's minds.

Newsweek, 27 April 1992

◆

Let me tell you a little about my extremism. I am extremely careful never to be extreme. I am extremely aware of the dangerous duplicity of Socialism, and extremely determined to turn back the tide before it destroys everything we hold dear. I am extremely disinclined to be deceived by the mask of moderation that Labour adopts whenever an election is in the offing, a mask now being worn by all those who would 'keep the red flag flying here'.

Conservative Party Conference, 14 October 1977

◆

We do not believe that if you cut back what Government does you diminish its authority. On the contrary, a Government that did less, and therefore did better, would strengthen its authority.

Conservative Party Conference, 14 October 1977

◆

The counterpart of the withdrawal of Government from interference in prices and profits in the private sector which both we and you want to see, is inevitably the withdrawal of Government from interference in wage bargaining. There can be no selective return to personal responsibility.

Speech to Scottish industrialists, January 1978

◆

There are still people in my party who believe in consensus politics. I regard them as quislings, as traitors... I mean it.

1978

◆

We must learn again to be one nation, or one day we shall be no nation.

1978

◆

The National Health Service will not be privatised. The National Health Service was never going to be privatised. No matter what the emergency, accident or disease; no matter how long or complicated the treatment, the Health Service is there, the Health Service will always be there, to provide the finest care. There to heal, there to cure and there to tend the needs of the patient.

On the NHS, 13 November 1989

◆

The decade and the century which open up before us must see the lasting triumph of liberty, our common cause. The world needs Britain – and Britain needs us – to make that happen.

Conservative Party Conference, 13 November 1989

◆

Sound policies are sound for all times.

16 November 1987

◆

Today it seems as if people are made to feel guilty about being well off. But Christ did not condemn riches as such, only the way in which they were used and those who put their trust in them.

March 1978

◆

A man may climb Everest for himself, but at the summit he plants his country's flag.

14 October 1988

◆

This country belongs to the courageous, not the timid.

The Times, September 1978

◆

We have strong policies founded on strong principles and a record of success and an international reputation and country after country following our policies as they come in and say to me: 'We have tried everything else, now we will try Thatcherism!' and I say to them: 'Thatcherism is much older than me. It is based on fundamental common sense, the limitation of the power of Government and handing more and more powers and the fruits of their work back to people!' and it works! That is what matters.

28 October 1989

◆

If we went on as we are then by the end of the century there would be four million people of the New Commonwealth and Pakistan here. Now, that is an awful lot and I think it means that people are really rather afraid that this country might be rather swamped by people with a different culture and, you know, the British character has done so

much for democracy and law, and done so much throughout the world, that if there is any fear that it might be
swamped, people are going to be really rather hostile to
those coming in. So, if you want good race relations you
have got to allay people's fears on numbers.

Granada TV, January 1978

◆

I have never filled in a pools coupon, so I have never been
a winner. But I am going to have a shot from now on.

Following victory in the vote of no confidence in the Callaghan
Government, 25 March 1979

◆

Let us make this country safe to work in. Let us make this
country safe to walk in. Let us make it a country safe to
grow up in. Let us make it a country safe to grow old in.

In a party political broadcast, 30 April 1979

◆

I must warn you, that although our party is going to win
overall, I could lose Finchley.

To her family on the eve of the election in May 1979 (she won,
almost doubling her majority)

◆

Our first duty to liberty is to keep our own. But it is also our duty – as Europeans – to keep alive in the eastern as well as the western half of our continent those ideas of human dignity which Europe gave to the world.

Let us therefore resolve to keep the lamps of freedom burning bright so that all who look to the West from the shadows of the East need not doubt that we remain true to those human spiritual values that lie at the heart of European civilisation.

The Times, 25 June 1977

◆

Life in a free society ... is heaven on earth to life in a Socialist society such as Russia.

House of Commons, 5 June 1986

◆

The cuts are not divisive. Too much state spending is divisive. It divides the honest saver from the profligate spender. It favours those who live for the day rather than those who provide for the morrow.

Speech at Conservative Women's Conference, 21 May 1980

◆

We have done quite a lot fundamental with steel. Seventy thousand redundancies. All right, it has cost us a bit.

Sunday Times, 3 May 1981

◆

I am much nearer to creating one nation than Labour will ever be. Socialism is two nations. The privileged rulers, and everyone else. And it always gets to that. What I am desperately trying to do is create one nation with everyone being a man of property, or having the opportunity to be a man of property.

Sunday Times, 27 February 1983

◆

To me, consensus seems to be: the process of abandoning all beliefs, principles, values, and policies in search of something in which no one believes, but to which no one objects; the process of avoiding the very issues that need to be solved, merely because you cannot get agreement on the way ahead. What great cause would have been fought and won under the banner 'I stand for consensus'?

The Downing Street Years, 1993

◆

Liberty and property are intricately bound up in our history; and a country that has no property right has no human rights... You cannot have freedom without capital and private property in the hands of the people.

Reader's Digest, January 1984

◆

My main reason for hope lies in the character of the British people. We've always shown great industrial ability and enterprise. We've always been outward looking. From Elizabethan times this country has thrived because the people have gone overseas seeking trade; so I believe we have a world perspective.

Reader's Digest, January 1984

◆

People from my sort of background needed grammar schools to compete with children from privileged homes like Shirley Williams and Anthony Wedgwood Benn.

Conservative Party Conference, 1977

◆

One of the delegates to the Labour Party Conference was loudly applauded when he called the police 'the enemy'. Enemy? The overwhelming majority of the British people regard the police as friends: they admire and are deeply thankful for their courage and the courage of their families.

Conservative Party Conference, 11 October 1985

◆

Unless we change our ways and our direction, our greatness as a nation will soon be a footnote in the history books, a distant memory of an offshore island, lost in the mists of time like Camelot, remembered kindly for its noble past.

2 May 1979

◆

I can't bear Britain in decline. I just can't.

27 April 1979

◆

I think we have gone through a period when too many children and people have been given to understand 'I have a problem, it is the Government's job to cope with it!' or 'I have a problem, I will go and get a grant to cope with it!' 'I am homeless, the Government must house me!' and so they are casting their problems on society and who is society? There is no such thing! There are individual men and women and there are families and no Government can do anything except through people and people look to themselves first. It is our duty to look after ourselves and then also to help look after our neighbour and life is a reciprocal business and people have got the entitlements too much in mind without the obligations, because there is no such thing as an entitlement unless someone has first met an obligation.

Woman's Own, 23 September 1987

◆

A responsible society is one in which people do not leave it to the person next door to do the job. It is one in which people help each other. Where parents put their children first. Friends look out for the neighbours, families for their elderly members. That is the starting point for care and support – the unsung efforts of millions of individuals, the selfless work of thousands upon thousands of volunteers. It is their spirit that helps to bind our society together. They've made Britain envied the world over for the strength of its voluntary contribution. Caring isn't measured by what you say: It's expressed by what you do.

Conservative Women's Conference, 1986

◆

I wish to goodness more people would in fact take responsibility for looking after their own families instead of expecting others to look after them. It is not selfish. It is not selfish to have an ambition, to want to do more for your own family so that they have a better way of life than you had. It is not selfish to want to have enough over to help your own parents. It is not selfish to wish to benefit from your own efforts so that you may then have money over to give to causes which you choose or to choose a lifestyle and a way of life which you wish to choose. There is nothing selfish about that. Indeed, when I hear people talking about materialism, I say that it is not making the money that counts but it is what you do with it. It is there in which you demonstrate the human spirit and demonstrate the things which made this country great.

Speech to the Centre for Policy Studies AGM, 28 April 1988

◆

The mission of this Government is much more than the promotion of economic progress. It is to renew the spirit and solidarity of the nation.

6 June 1979

◆

If a woman like Eva Perón with no ideals can get that far, think how far I can go with all the ideals I have.

Sunday Times, 1980

◆

It is an absolute mystery to me how it is possible to do eleven years at school with teachers who are graduates, who are responsible people, and still come out without knowing properly the English language, literature, mathematics, a certain amount of science, a good general knowledge, and proper history and geography. Most people want young people to be taught the best things about our country. We have a great deal to do there.

28 April 1988

◆

Iron entered my soul. You need a touch of steel. Otherwise you become like India Rubber.

BBC Radio, March 1980

◆

My politics are based ... on things I and millions like me were brought up with. An honest day's work for an honest day's pay; live within your means; put by a nest-egg for a rainy day; pay your bills on time; support the police.

1981

◆

The National Health Service is safe with us... The principle that adequate healthcare should be provided for all regardless of ability to pay must be the function of any arrangements for financing the NHS. We stand by that.

Conservative Party Conference, October 1982

◆

The very existence of the state, with its huge capacity for evil, is a potential threat to all the moral, cultural, social and economic benefits of freedom.

11 January 1996

◆

Some say I preach merely the homilies of housekeeping or the parables of the parlour. But I do not repent. Those parables would have saved many a financier from failure and many a country from crisis.

Lord Mayor's Banquet, 1982

◆

The spirit has stirred and the nation has begun to assert itself. Things are not going to be the same again.

◆

You can strike your way down, but you have to work your way up.

1983

◆

Power is a trust and we must exercise it in that way.

9 June 1983

◆

You can present people with ideas they may come to believe in, and as a result of them they will act, if they have the opportunities. Presenting people with opportunities is part of what politics is about.

If a political leader floats an idea five years ahead of its time he could kill that idea. But if it's two years ahead of its time it could work.

◆

Young people ought not to be idle. It's very bad for them.

The Times, 1984

◆

I came to office with one deliberate intent – to change Britain from a dependent to a self-reliant society, from a give-it-to-me to a do-it-yourself nation, to a get-up-and-go instead of a sit-back-and-wait Britain.

The Times, 8 February 1984

◆

In the Conservative Party we have no truck with outmoded Marxist doctrine about class warfare. For us it is not who you are, who your family is or where you come from that matters, but what you are and what you can do for your country that counts.

1984

◆

Yes, unemployment breeds frustration, but it's an insult to the unemployed to suggest that a man who doesn't have a job is likely to break the law.

Conservative Party Conference, 11 October 1985

◆

No one would remember the Good Samaritan if he'd only had good intentions. He had money as well.

1986

◆

The Communist creed set out to be equal for all people. It has turned out to have the greatest inequalities in it of any society today. You cannot have liberty and equality in the sense that you all have the same standard of living. If you go out for liberty you are giving people to use their talents and abilities according to how they have them. In doing so they will prosper not only themselves, but they'll produce jobs and an increased standard of living for others. So you can't have liberty and equality in the sense of material equality. You can have liberty and equality in the sense that all have equal rights, all are equally important, all different, all with different talents. What you can have is liberty and fraternity. Now, it is the fraternity, the voluntarily helping people, as well as having your National Health Service and your pensioners. And do you know, if you look back to the Beveridge Report he did not attempt to substitute state help for voluntary help in any way. He gave state help yes, but added to it there must be plenty of scope for voluntary help and personal self-reliance. So you can have liberty and fraternity.

On liberty vs equality, 5 June 1983

◆

I believe in the acceptance of personal responsibility, freedom of choice, and the British Empire, which took freedom and the rule of law to countries which would never have known it otherwise.

The Times, 18 February 1983

◆

I shall be a radical Prime Minister for my second term of office because I am radically right.

Director, September 1983

◆

A determination to stick with the task of making Britain a more hospitable climate for freedom and enterprise would be, I feel, a good resolution for 1984 – and the rest of the decade.

Reader's Digest, January 1984

◆

But if I were the odd one out and I were right, that would not matter, would it?

The Times, 14 June 1986 (when asked what her view would be if sanctions against South Africa were the only way to keep the Commonwealth together)

◆

If you do not have stars to steer by, a fixed point in the heavens and a compass to guide you, you will then become merely the slave of your in-tray.

◆

A responsible society is one in which people do not leave it to the person next door to do the job. It is one in which people help each other, where parents put their children first, friends look out for neighbours, families for their elderly members, that is the starting point for care and support – the unsung efforts of millions of individuals, the selfless work of thousands upon thousands of volunteers. Caring isn't measured by what you say, it's expressed by what you do.

Conservative Women's Conference, 1986

◆

Governments have a duty to show the way ahead. They must give leadership – as this Government has done and intends to go on doing. But the power to bring results lies with the men of enterprise, the manufacturers, the financiers and the businessmen who deal with the real products of real industries. Responsibility for securing our prosperity lies heavily on all of us and on our colleagues and co-workers at every level throughout the country. Without that prosperity, and the political and social stability which goes with it, Britain would have little influence in the world.

Lord Mayor's Banquet, 12 November 1979

◆

Popular capitalism is on the march... Of course, there will always be people who, in the name of morality, sneer at this and call it 'materialism'. But isn't it moral that people should want to improve the material standard of living, of their families, by their own effort? Isn't it moral that families should work for the means to look after their old folk? Isn't it moral that people should save, so as to be responsible for themselves?... And it is for Government to work with that grain in human nature to strengthen the strand of responsibility and independence: it benefits the family; it benefits the children; it is the essence of freedom.

Scottish Conservative Party Conference, May 1987

◆

It would be fatal for us to stand just where we are now. What would be our slogan for the 1990s if we did that? Would 'consolidate' be the word that we stitch on our banners? Whose blood would run faster at the prospect of five years of consolidation?

Speech to the Conservative Party Conference, 9 October 1987

◆

Now one or two things have changed since 1975. In that year we were still groaning under Labour's so-called 'social contract'. People said we should never be able to govern again. Remember how we had all been lectured about political impossibility? You couldn't be a Conservative, and sound like a Conservative, and win an election – they said. And you certainly couldn't win an election and then act like a Conservative and win another election. And – this was absolutely beyond dispute – you couldn't win two elections and go on behaving like a Conservative, and yet win a third election.

Conservative Party Conference, 1987

◆

Fear is not the basis for foreign policy.

◆

Interviewer: We hear of Thatcherism. What does it mean? Prime Minister: It is not a name that I created in the sense of calling it an 'ism'. Let me tell you what it stands for. It stands for sound finance and Government running the affairs of the nation in a sound financial way. It stands for honest money – not inflation. It stands for living within your means. It stands for incentives because we know full well that the growth, the economic strength of the nation comes from the efforts of its people. Its people need incentives to work as hard as they possibly can. All that has produced economic growth.

It stands for something else. It stands for the wider and wider spread of ownership of property, of houses, of shares, of savings. It stands for being strong in defence – a reliable ally and a trusted friend. People call those things

Thatcherism; they are, in fact, fundamental common sense and having faith in the enterprise and abilities of the people. It was my task to try to release those. They were always there; they have always been there in the British people, but they couldn't flourish under Socialism. They have now been released. That's all that Thatcherism is.

◆

Sir Robin Day: Under Thatcherism – your critics say – the nation is not one nation but a divided nation.
Prime Minister: Let me answer that very deeply because I feel very strongly about it. The greatest division this nation has ever seen were the conflicts of trade unions towards the end of a Labour Government – terrible conflicts. That trade union movement then was under the diktat of trade union bosses, some of whom are still there. They used their power against their members. They made them come out on strike when they didn't want to. They loved secondary picketing. They went and demonstrated outside companies where there was no dispute whatsoever, and sometimes closed them down. They were acting as they were later in the coal strike, before my whole trade union laws were brought through by this Government. They were out to use their power to hold the nation to ransom, to stop power from getting to the whole of manufacturing industry to damage people's jobs, to stop power from getting to every house in the country, power, heat and light to every housewife, every child, every school, every pensioner. You want division; you

want conflict; you want hatred. There it was. It was that which Thatcherism – if you call it that – tried to stop. Not by arrogance, but by giving power to the ordinary, decent, honourable, trade union member who didn't want to go on strike. By giving power to him over the Scargills of this world.

That is one conflict. That has gone. Another one. I believe passionately that people have a right, by their own efforts, to benefit their own families, so we have taken down taxation. It doesn't matter to me who you are or what your background is. If you want to use your own efforts to work harder – yes, I am with you all the way, whether it is unskilled effort or whether it is skilled, we have taken the income tax down.

The third thing. All my predecessors – yes, I agree, Disraeli; yes, Harold Macmillan – I would say I am right in their tradition. It was Disraeli's one nation. We have had an increase in home ownership – the heart of the family under this Government.

Sir Robin Day: Can I ask another question, Prime Minister?

Prime Minister: You asked me the most fundamental question.

Sir Robin Day: We are not having a party political broadcast, we are having an interview so I have to ask some questions occasionally.

Prime Minister: You asked, what I know you call the gut question. Right. It's gone for the jugular. Let me finish it. More home ownership; far more share ownership; far more savings in building society accounts. This is what is building one nation – as every earner becomes a shareholder, as more and more people own their homes. No. We are getting rid of the divisions. We are replacing conflict with cooperation. We are building one nation through wider property-owning democracy.

BBC *Panorama* interview, 8 June 1987

◆

Ours is a creed which travels and endures. Its truths are written in the human heart. It is the faith which once more has given life to Britain and offers hope to the world. We pledge in this party to uphold these principles of freedom and to fight for them. We pledge it to our allies overseas, and we pledge it to this country we are proud to serve.

The conclusion of Margaret Thatcher's final speech to a Conservative Party Conference, 12 October 1990

◆

If you have a good Thatcher, you keep your home water- and wind-proof.

Interview with Barbara Walters, February 1991

◆

Given time, it would have been seen as one of the most far-reaching and beneficial reforms ever made in the working of local government.

On the Community Charge (Poll Tax), 1993

◆

The legal system we have and the rule of law are far more responsible for our traditional liberties than any system of one man one vote. Any country or Government which wants to proceed towards tyranny starts to undermine legal rights and undermine the law.

Conservative Party Conference, October 1966

◆

There is no Government in the free world which can guarantee everyone a job. I want to make that absolutely clear. Yes, you could guarantee everyone a job – in a Soviet society by total direction of labour. You do what you are told to do and you don't have a chance of anything else. You go where you are told to go and you don't have a chance to go anywhere else. You haven't got any human rights and so on and so forth. It's in that society you can guarantee everyone a job. It wouldn't be the sort of society worth living in.

8 June 1987

◆

I call the Conservative Party now to a crusade. Not of the Conservative Party. I appeal to all those men and women of good will who do not want a Marxist future for themselves or their children or their children's children.

For this is not just a fight about national solvency. It is a fight about the very foundations of the social order. It is a crusade not merely to put a temporary block on Socialism but to stop its onwards march once and for all.

The Times, 9 October 1976

•

In other words, I want to get totally rid of class distinction. As someone put it in one of the papers this morning: Marks and Spencer have triumphed over Karl Marx and Engels.

The Times, 6 May 1985

•

I want a capital-earning democracy. Every man and woman a capitalist. Housing is the start. If you're a man or woman of property, you've got something. So every man a capitalist, and every man a man of property.

The Observer, 8 May 1983

•

What stands in our way? The prospects of another winter of discontent? I suppose it might, but I prefer to believe that certain lessons have been learnt from experience, that we are coming slowly, painfully to an autumn of understanding. I hope it will be followed by a winter of common sense.

Speech to the Conservative Party Conference, 10 October 1980

◆

Freedom under the law must never be taken for granted.
1975

◆

I hope to be Prime Minister one day and I do not want
there to be one street in Britain I cannot go down.
1 May 1977

◆

Citizenship should be based on those who have a close and
real relationship with this country and its inhabitants.
The Times, 4 November 1976

◆

Prime Ministers must learn to live with criticism. After
all – and despite the occasional strong temptation –
Prime Ministers can no longer have those with whom
they disagree taken out of circulation.
12 November 1979

◆

Sometimes we have to prescribe unpleasant and even
painful remedies: but that is because we really care about

curing the disease that has afflicted Britain. We want to restore her to full strength again.

12 November 1979

◆

Modern liberty rests upon three pillars. They are: representative democracy; economic freedom; and the rule of law.

Winston Churchill Memorial Lecture, 18 October 1979

◆

Since we last met there have been one or two changes on the political scene. On that occasion, as you so aptly remarked, I spoke to you as Leader of the Opposition. I am very pleased with my promotion to Prime Minister. I much prefer this job to the other.

Conservative Party Conference, 1979

◆

On behalf of the Government to which you have given the task of leading this country out of the shadows let me close with these words: You gave us your trust. Be patient. We shall not betray that trust.

Conservative Party Conference, 1979

◆

There are those who say our nation no longer has the stomach for the fight. I think I know our people and I know they do.

16 October 1981

◆

In overcoming the problems which face this country, we shall need to draw upon all the strengths of one nation. But even that will not be enough, for all our interests lead us towards the creation of one world. And everything which we have learnt and experienced makes us determined to work for one free world. That is our history. That is our destiny.

Lord Mayor's Banquet, 16 November 1981

◆

We Conservatives don't duck the difficult issues. We face them determined to overcome them.

◆

We are in the business of planting trees, for our children and grandchildren, or we have no business to be in politics at all. We are not a one-generation party. We do not intend to let Britain become a one generation society. Let us not forget the lesson of history. The long term always starts today.

8 October 1982

◆

The only way we can achieve great things for Britain is by asking great things of Britain. We will not disguise our purpose, nor betray our principles. We will do what must be done. We will tell the people the truth and the people will be our judge.

Conservative Party Conference, 1982

◆

As in England and Scotland, so in Wales, the Conservatives are the party of the future. It is we who bring the new industries to the Valleys. It is we who bring new opportunities to families to do the best for themselves and for their country. And we bring a new chance to the nation to fulfil its destiny – a free people, a great people, proud of their past, ready to adapt to the future.

Speech in Cardiff, 1983

◆

Visions do not become a reality overnight, or even in four years. They have to be worked for, consistently, unswervingly. We have set a true course – a course that is right for the character of Britain, right for the people of Britain and right for the future of Britain. To that course we shall hold fast. We shall see it through – to success.

Conservative Party Conference, 1983

◆

Human progress is not automatic. Civilisation has its ebbs and flows, but if we look at the history of the last five hundred years, whether in the field of art, science, technology, religious tolerance or in the practice of politics, the conscious inspiration of it all has been the belief and practice of freedom under law; freedom disciplined by morality, under the law perceived to be just.

Speech to Joint Houses of Congress, 20 February 1985

◆

In a democracy nothing but nothing justifies a resort to violence. People are entitled to look to their Government to defend them against those who have recourse to it.

Speech at the Lord Mayor's Banquet, 11 November 1985

◆

It is Government's job to maximise the liberty of the people under a rule of law and therefore to make your Government systems serve the liberty of the people, and not to extinguish them. In other words, the Government is servant of the people and not their master.

8 July 1986

◆

I am far more interested in achieving the things in which I believe in than I am in my own personal future. Far more interested.

8 July 1986

◆

Interviewer: Will this be your last general election as leader of the Conservatives?
MT: I would hope not, I would hope not. This is only the third term we are asking for. There is quite a long way to go.

11 May 1987

◆

The other thing is trying to make certain that everyone does have the opportunity to develop their talents, and this is why I speak as I do about children who do not have and why we are putting so much emphasis on education.

Woman's Own, 23 September 1987

◆

All too often the ills of this country are passed off as those of society. Similarly, when action is required, society is called upon to act. But society as such does not exist except as a concept. Society is made up of people. It is people who have duties and beliefs and resolve. It is people who get things done.

Sunday Times, 10 July 1988

◆

May I then go on to the immense task that I still think needs to be done? It is interesting now that people obviously, fortunately, are trying to point out the fruits of what we have done. What I still think needs to be done is to go back once again to propound the fundamental beliefs that led us along that path in the first place, because we are all here not merely because we believe in a miscellaneous collection of policies but because we believe that those policies are founded upon certain principles.

28 April 1988

◆

My worry now is that sometimes we are talking about policies without talking about the underlying principles and beliefs which are absolutely vital to their continuation.

28 April 1988

◆

Freedom of speech is freedom to say what other people disagree with, not merely things which are anodyne.

28 April 1988

◆

Choice is the essence of ethics. If there were no choice there would be no ethics, no good, no evil. Good and evil only have meaning in so far as man is free to choose.

    1977

◆

If someone is confronting our essential liberties, if someone is inflicting injuries and harm, by God I'll confront them!

    1979

◆

We intend freedom and justice to conquer. Yes, we do have a creed and we wish others to share it. But it is not part of our policy to impose our beliefs by force or threat of force.

    September 1983

◆

We must try to find ways to starve the terrorist or the hijacker of the oxygen of publicity on which they depend.

    Speech to the American Bar Association, 15 July 1985

◆

Of course you have a duty to show the disfigurations of society as well as its more agreeable aspects. But if TV in the western world uses its freedom continually to show all that is worst in our society, while the centrally controlled television of the Communist world and the dictatorships show only what is judged advantageous to them and suppress everything else, how are the uncommitted to judge between us? How can they fail to misjudge if they view matters only through a distorted mirror?

To an audience of television producers

◆

I am not one who, to quote an American author, believes that democracy and enterprise have finally won the battle of ideas – that we have therefore arrived at the end of history, and there is nothing left to fight for. That would be unutterably complacent, indeed foolish. There will always be threats to freedom, not only from frontal assaults, but more insidiously by erosion from within.

The Independent, 14 November 1989

◆

I am an undiluted admirer of American values and the American dream and I believe they will continue to inspire not just the people of the United States but millions across the face of the globe.

Speech to the Aspen Institute, Colorado, 5 August 1990

◆

The world has seen many revolutions. Some at the time have been hailed as great advances. Now they are considered by many to have been great tragedies. But the true revolution – the revolution of freedom which is sweeping the world today – is one which should cause all of us only joy. Not joy because one side or another has won. But joy because all mankind has won. For Man was created to enjoy the dignity of freedom. This is the conviction which has sustained me in a lifetime of politics. And I hope that it is a conviction which may sustain you too. For it is your generation which must carry the torch of freedom forward.

Speech to Leningrad State University, 29 May 1991

♦

For me, so long as Britain is true to herself – with the freedom to decide for herself what is best for herself – she will always be Great Britain.

26 September 1995

♦

The idea that men must govern themselves not by the arbitrary commands of a ruler but by their own considered judgement is the means whereby chaos is replaced by order, violence by the peaceful resolution of differences, and tyranny by freedom.

7 December 1999

◆

Liberty is a plant of slow growth and one that demands constant and careful attention. Yet there seems to be an inevitability about it, for liberty is man's natural and desired condition.

7 December 1999

◆

Creating the practical circumstances in which freedom can flourish requires more than the mere parroting of empty phrases like 'human rights'.

7 December 1999

◆

The events of September 11 are a terrible reminder that freedom demands eternal vigilance. And for too long we have not been vigilant. We have harboured those who hated us, tolerated those who threatened us and indulged those who weakened us.

11 February 2002

◆

The fundamental role of Government in a free society is to create a framework where the talents and abilities of the people can flourish. I remember once comparing this framework with another frame – the one which surrounds a picture. You need that frame, certainly: but it mustn't over-shadow the painting itself – for that's where the true worth really lies.

Message to Chapman University Conference, 4 May 2002

◆

Today, some find it all too easy to forget the sufferings of those years. Just as Communism had many apologists who sought to blind us its horrors and failures, so there are people who now talk almost nostalgically about the past and deride all that has been achieved over the last two decades. Our duty is to remember and remind. To forget the past would dishonour all those who fought heroically to resist Communism's evil – it would also place us in danger of repeating its mistakes.

Message to the Prague Conference on European Conscience and Communism, 30 May 2008

ON PERSONALITY AND POLITICS

You don't tell deliberate lies, but sometimes you have to be evasive.

1976

◆

I have changed everything.

1976

◆

My great fear is that when the time comes, I might fail.

April 1977

◆

I've got no hang-ups about my background, like you intellectual commentators in the south-east. When you're actually doing things, you don't have time for hang-ups.

1977

◆

There are a few times when I get home at night and everything has got on top of me when I shed a few tears, silently, alone.

1978

◆

It is not the business of politicians to please everyone.

29 January 1978

◆

The reason I am in politics is because I believe in certain things and try to put them into practice.

◆

We are not in politics to ignore people's worries, we are in politics to deal with them.

◆

Many of our troubles are due to the fact that our people turn to politicians for everything.

◆

If I lose, I will be out tomorrow.

Day before the 1979 general election

◆

Where there is discord may we bring harmony. Where there is error, may we bring truth. Where there is doubt, may we bring faith. And where there is despair, may we bring hope.

Quoting St Francis of Assisi on the steps of 10 Downing Street, May 1979

◆

To accuse me of being inflexible is absolute poppycock.

28 October 1981

◆

I hope the one quality I am not lacking is courage.

November 1979

◆

I was on *The Jimmy Young Show*, he played an Andy Williams song for me and the song was 'The Other Side of Me'. Well there are two sides of me – the informal, friendly me and the iron touch, the Iron Lady.

Daily Mail, May 1980

◆

Deep in their instincts, they [the majority of people] find what I am saying and doing right, and I know it is because that is the way I was brought up. I'm eternally grateful for the way I was brought up in a small town. We knew everyone, we knew what people felt. I sort of regard myself as a very normal, ordinary person with all the right instinctive antennae.

Sunday Times, 3 August 1980

◆

I said at the start I shall get things right in the end, and I shall.

Daily Express, August 1980

◆

To those waiting with bated breath for that favourite media catchphrase, the U-turn, I have only one thing to say. You turn if you want to. The Lady's not for turning.

Conservative Party Conference, 10 October 1980

◆

Oh, those poor shopkeepers.

Visiting Toxteth after the 1981 riots

◆

I do not believe that people who go on strike in this country have legitimate cause.

1982

◆

'Oh, Lord, teach me to learn that occasionally I make mistakes.'

Quoting her favourite poem, BBC Radio, 1982

◆

Victorian values were the values when our country became great.

1982

◆

I was asked whether I was trying to restore Victorian values. I said straight out I was. And I am.

1983

◆

I don't think I'm as good as you think.

1983

◆

If you are going to work for politicians you should remember that they have very large fingers and very large toes and you can tread upon them remarkably easily. I, however, have stubs.

◆

It's a result that will reverberate through our history. Its consequences will outlive most of us here tonight.

On the 1983 general election result, 7 June 1983

◆

It's got to be my ideas. Not every bit of draft is mine but I go through it all. First we do the ideas, they go away and draft, then that draft's usually torn up, then we do another one, and then I literally spend hours and hours going through that. We change it and change it, and some speeches we'd still be changing now, if we hadn't delivered them already.

On writing speeches, 9 June 1983

◆

Cecil, these have been such happy hours. We have done such a lot for the country together and we will do much more.

To Cecil Parkinson following his resignation from the Government over the Sara Keays affair

◆

If they do not wish to confer the honour, I am the last person who would wish to receive it.

On Oxford University's decision not to give her an honorary degree, 1985

◆

I may not be Prime Minister at six o'clock.

To colleagues just before the no confidence debate over Westland, 26 January 1986

◆

I know nothing about diplomacy, but I know I want certain things for Britain.

1986

◆

There is just one thing I would like to make clear. The rose I am wearing is the rose of England.

A dig at Labour's red rose logo, Conservative Party Conference, 1986

◆

I feel more genuine affection this time. I think I have become a bit of an institution and, you know, the sort of thing people expect to see around the place.

At the start of the general election campaign, May 1987

◆

I exercise my right as a free citizen to spend my own money in my own way, so that I can go on the day, the time, to the doctor I choose and get out fast.

On why she chose to use private healthcare, causing a political storm during the general election campaign, June 1987

◆

Margaret Thatcher: If people just drool and drivel they care, then I turn round and say, right, I also look to see what you actually do.

David Dimbleby: Why do you use the words drool and drivel they care, is that what you think saying that you care about people's lives amounts to?

MT: No, I don't. I'm sorry I used those words.

Interview on the BBC *Nine O'Clock News*, 10 June 1987

◆

We've got a big job to do in some of those inner cities, a really big job.

To party workers at Conservative Central Office, 12 June 1987

◆

Oh, I have lots of human weaknesses, who hasn't?

1987

♦

We were told our campaign wasn't sufficiently slick. We regard that as a compliment.

1987

♦

You cannot have my job and have had a vision, a dream, a will to turn Britain round, to live up to the best of herself, without being more than a chairman of a committee... A Prime Minister has a task of leadership. If the trumpet gives an uncertain sound, who shall prepare himself to the battle?... If one has a sense of purpose, they call that authoritarianism. It is totally false, but there you are... Success is not an attractive thing to many people – they do not like it. And, of course, some of them are snobs. They can never forgive me for coming from a very ordinary background. It does not bother me at all. I cannot stand snobbery of any kind.

Interview with Brian Walden, *Sunday Times*, 8 May 1988

♦

I'll stay until I'm tired of it. So long as Britain needs me, I shall never be tired of it.

◆

Obviously one isn't indestructible – quite.

1988

◆

I've seen and heard so many things on the BBC that infuriate me almost every day of the week – tendentious reporting, unfair comment, unbearable violence and vulgarity – that I hesitate to say yes when any part of the BBC asks me to do anything.

To George Urban, 29 June 1988

◆

We have become a grandmother.

To reporters outside 10 Downing Street, 1989

◆

MT: I am staying my own sweet reasonable self, founded on very strong convictions which were a combination of reason and emotion. I feel passionately about personal liberty and Government is there to serve it. I feel passionately that it is the right of people to have more and more choice because I held these passionate convictions and fashioned our economic policies on them reasonably, firmly, strongly.

Interviewer: Prime Minister, I must stop you there!
MT: No, you must not!
Interviewer: I must! Thank you very much indeed!
Prime Minister: Strong leadership will continue!

The Walden Interview, 28 October 1989

◆

I am what I am.

29 November 1989

◆

I don't expect gratitude. No politician should do that.

1990

◆

Anything I want to keep quiet is normally in my handbag
so it is not left lying around. Things do not leak from my
handbag.

July 1990

◆

One is an ordinary person, and don't you forget it!

To Eve Pollard, 1991

◆

People who start things often don't see the end of them –
take Moses and the Promised Land.

1992

◆

I can be difficult and stubborn.

29 January 1994

ON APPEARANCE AND LIFESTYLE

You know how it is, if your hair looks awful, you feel awful.

Daily Mail, July 1965

◆

I don't want to give my life over to politics. I don't think I'd have the ability and I'd never be given the chance.

On the possibility of becoming Prime Minister, *Sunday Times*, March 1967

◆

Most of us have stopped using silver every day.

1970

◆

I'm not hard, I'm frightfully soft, but I will not be hounded ... I can jolly well stick up for myself.

Daily Mail, February 1972

◆

My hats seem to incense some people.

Daily Mail, February 1972

◆

Do I look bedraggled, woebegone, in a state of shock? At some stage I shall have to go to Elizabeth Arden to have the ravages repaired, but do you see signs of shock in my face? It's easier for a woman than a man to give up power because you are not so lost. I can fill the time by spring-cleaning the house.

Daily Mail, October 1974

◆

I'm a very good night worker.

1975

◆

I married at twenty-six. I knocked about a bit, as they say, and I was unhappy when my personal affairs did not go right. But I was never without hope for the future.

◆

I am worried about my image. I'm going to change it... I'm very aware that my image is important. I'm not at all pleased with the way I look on TV. I'm going to do something about it and the first thing is my hair. I'm going for the unkempt look.

Daily Mail, May 1976

◆

I'm not as posh as I sound. I'm not grand at all.

Daily Mirror, February 1977

◆

My greatest strength, I think, is that come what may I somehow cope.

◆

I'm going to have furniture I like ... because I intend to be there a long time.

BBC Radio, November 1977

◆

I do love an argument.

Daily Mail, February 1980

◆

I couldn't live without work. That's what makes me so sympathetic to these people who are unemployed. I don't know how they live without working.

News of the World, 4 May 1980

◆

I sort of regard myself as very normal.

◆

If you saw me at four o'clock in the morning with my make-up gone and running my hands through my hair you'd get a different picture.

August 1980

◆

I haven't the figure for jeans.

1980

◆

Failure? The possibilities don't exist.

On the Falklands War, 1982

◆

Mr Parkinson, they tell me you have influence with the Prime Minister. She must take a proper holiday and if you will speak to her about it so will I!

Her Majesty the Queen to Cecil Parkinson, 1983

◆

I'm sure I've made quite a number [of mistakes]. I don't think I could just suddenly say what they are now.

BBC Radio 4, 30 March 1983

◆

Look at a day when you are supremely satisfied at the end. It's not a day when you lounge around doing nothing; it's when you've had everything to do and you've done it.

◆

Of course it's the same old story. Truth usually is the same old story.

◆

I am extraordinarily patient – provided that I get my own way in the end.

1989

ON THE SEXES

If you want anything said, ask a man. If you want anything done, ask a woman.

May 1964

◆

No woman in my time will be Prime Minister or Foreign Secretary – not the top jobs. Anyway I wouldn't want to be Prime Minister. You have to give yourself one hundred per cent to the job.

1969

◆

I usually make up my mind about a man in ten seconds, and I very rarely change it.

1970

◆

It will be years, and not in my time, before a woman will lead the party or become Prime Minister.

1974

◆

I owe nothing to women's lib.

The Observer, December 1974

◆

It may be the cock that crows, but it is the hen that lays the eggs.

◆

I don't like strident women.

◆

I like to be made a fuss of by a lot of chaps.

Daily Mirror, February 1975

◆

I have a woman's ability to stick to a job and get on with it when everyone else walks off and leaves it.

16 February 1975

◆

Part of me is a woman and part of me is a politician. The MPs voted for the whole of me.

February 1975

◆

I cannot easily foresee the time when we have a woman Minister of Defence. But it would give me enormous joy to have the Navy singing 'There is Nothing Like a Dame'.

April 1975

◆

You cannot go so far up the ladder, and then not go to the limit, just because you are a woman.

◆

One does wish that there were a few more women in Parliament. Then one could be less conspicuous oneself.

◆

I don't notice that I'm a woman. I regard myself as the Prime Minister.

March 1980

◆

Ronald Reagan: Margaret, he [Pierre Trudeau] had no business talking to you like that, he was way out of line.
Margaret Thatcher: Oh, women know when men are being childish.

◆

The battle for women's rights has been largely won.

Conservative Party Conference, 1982

◆

One of the things being in politics has taught me is that men are not a reasoned or reasonable sex.

◆

When a woman is strong she is strident. If a man is strong he is a good guy.

October 1990

◆

Most women defend themselves – it is the female of the species – it is the tigress and lioness in you which tends to defend when attacked.

◆

True gentlemen deal with others for what they are, not for who their fathers were.

HUC TV, 1993

◆

In general, more nonsense was written about the so-called 'feminine factor' during my time in office than just about anything else. I was always asked how it felt to be a woman Prime Minister. I would reply: 'I don't know, I've never experienced the alternative.'

The Downing Street Years, 1993

◆

My experience is that a number of the men I have dealt with in politics demonstrate precisely those characteristics which they attribute to women – vanity and an inability to make tough decisions. There are also certain types of men who simply cannot abide working for women... Of course, in the eyes of the 'wet' Tory establishment I was not only a woman, but 'that' woman, someone not just of a different sex, but of a different class, a person with an alarming conviction that the values and virtues of middle England should be brought to bear on the problems which the establishment consensus had created. I offended on many counts.

The Downing Street Years, 1993

◆

I sometimes tell American audiences, Ma'am, that a wiser monarch than your predecessor, and a better Prime Minister than mine – two women ideally – would have managed to avoid that fateful tea party in Boston Harbour. Women are rather good at handling tea parties.

16 October 1995

ON DENIS AND THE FAMILY

When Denis asked me to be his wife, I thought long and hard about it. I had so much set my heart on politics that I hadn't really figured marriage in my plans. I had pushed it to the back of my mind and assumed it would occur of its own accord at some time in the future. I know that Denis too, because his wartime marriage had ended in divorce, asked me to be his wife only after much reflection. But the more I considered it, the surer I was. There was only one possible answer.

The Downing Street Years, 1993

◆

Denis's money got me on my way.

1983

◆

She stood twice for Dartford and the second time she cried on my shoulder I married her.

Denis Thatcher

◆

Denis has his own life and work and that's been very important to the both of us. He's not my second fiddle. He's first fiddle of his own orchestra. In fact he's his own conductor.

Daily Express, 20 February 1986

◆

I can trust my husband not to fall asleep on a public platform and he usually claps in the right places.

◆

Several things, she's got a good pair of legs.

Denis Thatcher, in answer to a question on what attracted him to her

◆

Tory Party worker: Mr Thatcher, I understand you have a drink problem.
Denis Thatcher: Yes, madam, I have. There is never enough of it.

◆

Tory Party worker: Mr Thatcher, how do you spend your time?

Denis Thatcher: Well, when I'm not completely pissed I like to play a lot of golf.

◆

If we're not careful, we'll have a dead cow on our hands.

Denis Thatcher during the 1979 general election campaign, when his wife picked up a baby calf for a photo opportunity

◆

The desire to win is born in most of us. The will to win is a matter of training. The manner of winning is a matter of honour.

Denis Thatcher, quoted in *The Downing Street Years*, 1993

◆

The Falklands marked her soul and mine.

Denis Thatcher

◆

Congratulations Sweetie Pie, you've won. It's just the rules.

A tearful Denis Thatcher after the first round of the 1990 leadership election

◆

Denis Thatcher: [in tears] It's just the disloyalty of it all.
Carol Thatcher: Look Dad, what really matters now is Mum. It's going to be a hell of a shock and we have to support her. We have to do everything we can to make it easier.

Walking across Horse Guards Parade, 22 November, 1990

◆

After all she's done, I think this is an act of gutless treachery. As far as I'm concerned Tory is now a four-letter word.

Carol Thatcher to a journalist outside her home, 22 November 1990

◆

Oh Mum, it's me. I think you're a heroine [bursts into tears]. I don't know how you made that speech. It's just so awful what they've done – your party are complete shits.

Carol Thatcher, speaking to her mother on the evening of 22 November 1990

◆

For forty years I have been married to one of the greatest women the world has ever produced. All I could produce – small as it may be – was love and loyalty.

◆

Carol Thatcher: Can you manage the supermarket shopping?
Margaret Thatcher: Good heavens, yes, dear, I've opened enough of them.

December 1990

◆

Isn't my mother wonderful, doing this for me and my son?

Mark Thatcher on his father's baronetcy, *Mail on Sunday*, 20 January 1991

◆

Mark has a hate–hate relationship with the press. He feels the press for years and years has given him a very hard time. Quite frankly he can't stand them and he finds it hard to disguise it. Mark has the full confidence of his mother. She really trusts him. When you've been through what she went through, when a number of people whom you thought you could trust, proved not quite so trustworthy, then to have somebody in whom you have total trust, is vitally important, and I think Mark has filled a very important role for her.

Cecil Parkinson, *World in Action*, 11 November 1991

◆

It's time to pay up for Mumsy.

Mark Thatcher, raising money from businessmen to set up the
Thatcher Foundation, 1991

◆

Duchess of York: Oh Denis, I do get an awful press, don't I?
Denis Thatcher: Yes, Ma'am. Has it occurred to you to
keep your mouth shut?

◆

Being the only girl in the world who can say that her
mother was Britain's first woman Prime Minister is
honour enough for me.

Carol Thatcher, 13 June 1992

◆

I now have to spell Thatcher when I make table reserva-
tions at restaurants – but I can cope with that.

Carol Thatcher, *The Independent*, 28 December 1993

◆

The idea that I run around peddling Kalashnikovs or second
hand MiG jets is ridiculous. I haven't even sold a penknife.

Mark Thatcher

◆

You cannot think of Margaret without Denis. There comes a time when every Prime Minister needs someone to give him or her the unvarnished truth, and, in Denis, Margaret had just that.

John Major, October 1995

ON SOCIALISM

I sometimes think the Labour Party is like a pub where the mild is running out. If someone does not do something soon, all that is left will be bitter and all that is bitter will be left.

1975

◆

In a Socialist society, parents should be seen and not heard.

Conservative Party Conference, 10 October 1975

◆

My job is to stop Britain going red.

The Times, March 1977

◆

What would they our ancestors think of Labour Britain today? A country in which people ask: 'Why work if you can get by without?'; 'Why do a good job when you will probably make out just as well if you do a bad one?'; 'Why bother to get extra qualifications when differentials and earnings so often depend on political muscle, not personal merit?'

Conservative Party Conference, 13 October 1978

◆

Mr Wedgwood Benn says that 'The forces of Socialism in Britain cannot be stopped.' They can be and they will be. We shall stop them. We shall stop them democratically, and I use the word in the dictionary sense, not the Bennite sense. What they cannot be is half stopped, least of all by those who for years helped to nurture and support them.

Conservative Party Conference, 1981

◆

And what a prize we have to fight for: no less than the chance to banish from our land the dark, divisive clouds of Marxist Socialism.

Scottish Conservative Party Conference, May 1983

◆

Socialism and Britain go ill together. It is not the British character.

Director, September 1983

◆

In the Falklands we had to fight the enemy without. Here the enemy is within and it is much more difficult to fight, but just as dangerous to liberty.

Speech to the 1922 Committee, referring to the miners, July 1984

◆

What we've got is an attempt to substitute the rule of the mob, for the rule of the law. It must not succeed.

On the miners' strike, 1984

◆

Scabs? They are lions!

On working miners, Conservative Party Conference, 13 October 1984

◆

I hate extremes of any kind. Communism and the National Front both seek the domination of the state over the individual. They both, I believe, crush the right of the individual. To me, therefore, they are parties of a similar kind. All my life I have stood against banning Communism or other extremist organisations because, if you do that, they go underground and it gives them an excitement that they don't get if they are allowed to pursue their policies openly. We'll beat them into the ground on argument... The National Front is a Socialist Front.

21 April 1978

◆

The problem with Socialism is that eventually you run out of other people's money.

◆

Some Socialists seem to believe that people should be numbers in a state computer. We believe they should be individuals. We are all unequal. No one, thank heavens, is like anyone else, however much the Socialists may pretend otherwise. We believe that everyone has the right to be unequal but to us every human being is equally important. A man's right to work as he will, to spend what he earns, to own property, to have the state as servant and not as master. They are the essence of a free economy. And on that freedom all our other freedoms depend.

Conservative Party Conference, 1975

◆

Liberty incurs responsibilities; that is why many people fear it, why many men fear it. Yes, some do fear it. Some would rather live on with the state deciding where you will live, what job you shall have, and do not forget there are some people – and this really is the essence of Communism and extreme left-wingism – who are that way because they want to control people's lives; first, because it gives them enormous power, and second, because they think that you can do it better. They forget that what happens in every society is it will dwarf and diminish people and if you come to a nation which dwarfs its citizens you will find that with small people no great things can be accomplished.

Interview with Hugo Young, 8 July 1986

♦

Labour supported that strike to the bitter end. Indeed, three months into the strike, Mr Kinnock told Mr Scargill publicly that there was no – and I quote – 'no alternative but to fight – all other roads are shut off'. What do you think would have happened if Mr Scargill had won? I think the whole country knows the answer. Neil would have knelt.

On Neil Kinnock's support of the miners' strike, 11 October 1985

♦

'To borrow and to borrow and to borrow' is not Macbeth with a heavy cold. It is Labour Party policy. But most people do not want to mortgage the future and leave their children to pick up the bill.

Conservative Party Conference, 11 October 1985

◆

Where Labour's pessimistic, we are full of hope. Where they are bitter, we are determined to succeed. Where they fear the future, we rise to the challenge and the excitement and the adventure. But then ours is the British way.

5 June 1983

◆

They haven't changed their Socialist spots. They've just changed their suits.

22 March 1992

◆

We were told you'll never stand a major industrial strike, let alone a coal strike. But we did just that. And we won.

Conservative Party Conference, 1985

◆

We must take with us into the 1990s the lessons of the decade we are leaving behind. And the overwhelming lesson is that Socialism has failed.

January 1990

◆

I am convinced that there is little force left in the original Marxist stimulus to revolution. Its impetus is petering out as the practical failure of the doctrine becomes daily more obvious. What is left is a technique of subversion and a collection of catchphrases. The former, the technique of subversion, is still dangerous. Like terrorism it is a menace that needs to be fought wherever it occurs.

Speech to the Foreign Policy Association, 18 December 1979

◆

I believe our way of life is infinitely superior for every human being than any which the Communist creed can offer.

The Times, 5 May 1980

◆

You know the critical thing with the Communist countries is Communism, which by definition consists of control by Government.

The Times, 31 January 1987

◆

I have here the Labour Party's manifesto. I'm told that a member of Labour's shadow Cabinet described it as 'the longest suicide note ever penned'. I can tell you this – If the British people were to put their signature to it, it would be a suicide note for Britain too.

1983

◆

What I was always surprised about was that some of those people, the SDP people, who if I might put it this way, hadn't the guts to stay within the Labour Party and fight within the Labour Party.

◆

The Labour Party won't die, the Labour Party will never die.

◆

Beneath its contrived self-confidence lies a growing certainty that the world and history has passed it by and that if Britain rejects it as I believe it will, Socialism must return forever to its proper place – the reading room of the British Library where Karl Marx found it – Section: history of ideas. Subsection: nineteenth century. Status: archaic.

Conservative Party Conference, October 1990

◆

Labour are still Socialist and they deliberately set out to impose more Government control over people's lives. That is where their whole belief starts. It starts with the power of Government over the lives of the people. That is the reason why they increase taxation – more power for them over our money, less power for the citizen. That is why they multiply controls and bureaucracy – more power for them, less for the wealth creators of our country. That is why they like nationalisation – more control over industry. That is why they reject privatisation and wider share ownership. That is why they want more council housing – because they want to have more control over the lives of the housing of the people and to use it for political purposes as in the Camdens and the Lambeths. That is why they oppose our plans for giving your doctors and nurses, your teachers and parents, more say, more responsibility, more power to decide near the point at which the decision has to be taken. That's why they oppose our plans for doing that in hospitals and in schools – they would rather have it decided by a bureaucratic level above. That is the essence of their creed – Government controls over the lives of the people – and it runs through all of their policies.

22 March 1992

◆

I would say of the [Tony Blair] Labour leader, as I once said of his [Neil Kinnock] predecessor: if it's that easy for him to give up the principles in which he DID believe, won't it be even easier for him to give up the principles in which he does NOT believe?

On Tony Blair, 8 October 1996

♦

Socialism is like one of those horrible viruses. You no sooner discover a remedy for one version, than it spontaneously evolves into another. In the past, there was nationalisation, penal taxation and the command economy. Nowadays Socialism is more often dressed up as environmentalism, feminism, or international concern for human rights. All sound good in the abstract. But scratch the surface and you'll as likely as not discover anti-capitalism, patronising and distorting quotas, and intrusions upon the sovereignty and democracy of nations. New slogans: old errors.

14 May 2003

ON THE WORLD STAGE

Every Conservative desires peace. The threat to peace comes from Communism which has powerful forces ready to attack anywhere. Communism waits for weakness, it leaves strength alone. Britain must therefore be strong, strong in her arms, strong in her faith, strong in her own way of life.

Margaret Roberts's election leaflet, 1950

◆

Ladies and Gentlemen, I stand before you tonight in my green chiffon evening gown, my face softly made up, my hair softly waved... The Iron Lady of the western world? Me? A Cold Warrior? Well, yes ... if that is how they wish to interpret my defence of the values and freedom fundamental to our way of life.

Referring to the Soviet magazine *Red Star* which was the first to call her the Iron Lady, 1976

◆

Perhaps this country needs an Iron Lady.

1977

◆

Marxists get up early to further their cause. We must get up even earlier to defend our freedom.

Daily Mail, May 1978

◆

Communism never sleeps, never changes its objectives. Nor must we.

Financial Times, May 1979

◆

There are forces more powerful and pervasive than the apparatus of war. You may chain a man, but you cannot chain his mind. You may enslave him, but you will not conquer his spirit. In every decade since the war Soviet leaders have been reminded that their pitiless ideology only survives because it is maintained by force. But the day will come when the anger and frustration of the people is so great that force cannot contain it. Then the edifice cracks; the mortar crumbles... One day, liberty will dawn on the other side of the wall.

In Berlin, 29 October 1982

◆

We are prepared to fight for peace.

1983

◆

We are the true peace movement.

1983

◆

We have invented weapons powerful enough to destroy the whole world. Others have created political systems evil enough to seek to enslave the whole world. Every free nation must face that threat. Every free nation must strain both to defend its freedom and to ensure the peace of the world.

Conservative Party Conference, 1982

◆

If you are pronouncing a new law that wherever Communism reigns against the will of the people, even though it's happened internally, there the United States shall enter, then we are going to have really terrible wars in the world.

Condemning the US invasion of Grenada, 1983

◆

If in the 1930s nuclear weapons had been invented and the Allies had been faced by Nazi SS20s and Backfire bombers, would it then have been morally right to have handed Hitler control of one of the most terrible weapons man has ever made? Would not that have been the one way to ensure that the thousand year Reich became exactly that? Would not unilateralism have given to Hitler the world domination he sought?

1983

◆

Nations overseas are applauding our new strength and resolve. They have found again their confidence in Britain. So long as we do not flinch from our responsibilities, neither they nor our people will be disappointed. We shall carry through the task that we have undertaken. There is no other way to success.

House of Commons, 20 November 1980

◆

I first became interested in Communism from reading about it when I was sixteen or seventeen. The thing which struck me very vividly was the total extinction of all personal liberty. I saw then that they had a world objective to dominate the world – which they pursued by one means or another. And this obviously never left me. It's not in the background of my mind, but in my bloodstream.

Daily Telegraph, December 1983

◆

I am an ally of the United States. We believe the same things, we believe passionately in the same battle of ideas, we will defend them to the hilt. Never try to separate me from them.

To Mikhail Gorbachev at their first meeting, 1984

◆

Britain is not just another country; it has never been just another country. We would not have grown into an Empire if we were just another European country with the size and strength that we were. It was Britain that stood when everyone else surrendered and if Britain pulls out of that commitment, it is as if one of the pillars of the temple has collapsed – because we are one of the pillars of freedom and, hitherto, everyone, including past Labour Prime Ministers, have known that Britain would stand and Britain had a nuclear weapon.

8 June 1987

◆

I am in step with the people of South Africa.

October 1989

◆

The fact is that we have had peace in Europe for, next year, forty years. That is a very long period of peace compared with previous periods, historically. I believe that the deterrence of nuclear weapons and the fact that their use would be so horrific has, in fact, helped to keep that peace.

22 December 1984

◆

If we let Iraq succeed, no small country can ever feel safe again. The law of the jungle takes over.

August 1990

◆

A bully has no respect for a weakling. And the way to stop a bully is not to be weak. The way to stop a bully for ever being a bully is to say, 'I'm as strong as you. Anything you do to me, I can do to you.'

The World This Weekend, 10 January 1982

◆

The obligations of democratic leaders are clear. They must know what principles they stand for. They must devise policies which implement those principles. They must proclaim both philosophy and policies in a way which is convincing to their electorates. Thereafter they must act – while avoiding the temptation to interfere where Government has nothing legitimate to say or do. Only then will the people of a free democracy follow where their leaders wish to go.

Winston Churchill Memorial Lecture, 18 October 1979

◆

Human beings have their own rights as human beings and I will not sink to the level of using them as bargaining counters.

Responding to Saddam Hussein's imprisonment of Western hostages, August 1990

◆

In my view dictators do not surrender. They have to be well and truly defeated.

Independent on Sunday, 20 January 1991

◆

The Russians are bent on world domination.

The Times, 20 January 1976

◆

While the Soviet Union has imposed its rule on its neighbours and drawn an iron curtain between East and West, we in Great Britain have given freedom and independence to more than forty countries whose populations

now number more than one thousand million – a quarter
of the world's total.

The Times, 30 September 1983

◆

The Russians put guns before butter. We put just about
everything before guns.

The Times, 20 January 1976

◆

To many of us it seems there is precious little difference
between the politics of the Communist Party and the
policies of the Labour Party.

The Times, 12 December 1980

◆

By 'they' I mean that somewhat strange alliance between
the comrades of the Russian Defence Ministry and our
Defence Ministry.

The Times, 2 February 1976

◆

Stop the excuses. Help Bosnia now.

New York Times, 6 August 1992

◆

Much of the evil which still stalks the world was planted and cultivated first by Communism.

5 November 1993

◆

This party is pro-American.

13 October 1984

◆

1989 will be remembered for decades to come as the year when half the people of half our continent began to throw off their chains. The messages on our banners in 1979 – freedom, opportunity, family, enterprise, ownership – are now inscribed on the banners in Leipzig, Warsaw, Budapest and even Moscow. For decades, East Germans had risked their lives to claw their way through the barbed wire to freedom. Now they come, not by the brave handful but by the cheerful thousand. Hungary, turning day by day more confidently towards freedom and dignity, dismantles Communism and opens her borders to the West. In Poland, the freely elected representatives of a courageous people, move resolutely into the seats of Government. And let us never forget Poland's contribution to our own Finest Hour. What happened in Russia in 1917 wasn't a revolution. It was a coup d'état. The true revolution is what is happening in Russia and eastern Europe today.

Conservative Party Conference, 13 October 1989

◆

Constitutions have to be written on hearts, not just paper.

Statecraft, 2003

◆

One lesson stands out: at times such as these – times of change, of hope and yet of danger – Britain's unique qualities are needed once again: steadfastness in defence; staunchness as an ally; and willingness always to give a lead. Time after time, when put to the test in a just cause, these qualities have served Britain and the world well. They will do so again.

Lord Mayor's Banquet, 12 November 1990

◆

Economic sanctions are not the way to promote peaceful change. Sanctions do not work. Indeed they make problems worse. They would be a blow to all those firms and people who are in the forefront of efforts to end apartheid by giving black Africans more jobs and greater opportunities.

On South African sanctions

◆

Terrorism has to be defeated; it cannot be tolerated or side-stepped.

◆

Terrorism exploits the natural reluctance of a free society to defend itself, in the last resort, with arms. Terrorism thrives on appeasement. Of course we shall continue to make every effort to defeat it by political means. But in this case that was not enough. The time had come for action. The United States took it. Its decision was justified, and, as friends and allies, we support it.

On the USA's bombing of Libya, 16 April 1986

◆

America is the flagship of freedom and she must sail into the sunrise, not look back at what may or may not have happened!

◆

I do not like apartheid. It is wrong. I like valuing people for what they are, not for their colour or their background.

Interview in *The Guardian*, 8 July 1986

◆

We see so many things in the same way and you can speak of a real meeting of minds. I feel no inhibitions about describing the relationship as very, very special.

On US–UK relations, *Financial Times*, 23 February 1985

◆

It is with friends you can talk frankly. Never with rancour. Always with friendship. Always with understanding. That is the way it is between Britain and the United States. And that is the way it will always be.

Daily Telegraph, 10 December 1983

◆

We are very fortunate to have some else's weapons stationed on our soil, to fight those targeted on us.

Time, 16 February 1981

◆

I do not understand the unilateralists. If they hated nuclear weapons as much as I do they would want them down in the world as a whole. I am the true disarmer. I keep peace and freedom and justice with it.

The Times, 17 January 1983

◆

Both the President and Mr Gorbachev have said that they want to see a world without nuclear weapons. I cannot see a world without nuclear weapons. Let me be practical about it. The knowledge is there to make them. So do not go too hard for that pie in the sky because, while everyone would like to see it, I do not believe it is going to come about.

The Times, 28 March 1986

◆

It is absolutely right that President Reagan considers SDI, and thank goodness people considered nuclear research before the last world war.

House of Commons, 17 February 1987

◆

Of course, I would actually fire it.

Response when asked if she would launch Polaris in the event of
a Soviet conventional attack in Europe, 1 June 1983

◆

MT: I hope to see it [Russia] as a fully democratic country, yes.

Interviewer: Under Mr Gorbachev's influence?

MT: Yes, I hope to see it a fully democratic country.

Interviewer: Really?

MT: You sound surprised! That is the aim, that is the aim. He started the whole revolution, it is a revolution towards freedom, but really tried to do it in the first place as reforming Communism. That is impossible, and so now he is going to a multiparty system and has of course been preaching a totally different philosophy. Communism is a philosophy that Governments' decisions are the only source of authority, they did not recognise human rights as coming from anything more fundamental than the state, which they do. So much has been changed.

Interview for the *Sunday Times*, 21 February 1990

◆

What city can be a better introduction to the 'new' India which is emerging? A new India which will play an increasingly powerful international role. I welcome that. And I believe that with India in the vanguard, the philosophy of liberty under the law will extend its influence and prevail.

Speech in Bombay, 4 October 1994

◆

Within the Islamic world the Soviet collapse undermined the legitimacy of radical secular regimes and gave an impetus to the rise of radical Islam. Radical Islamist movements now constitute a major revolutionary threat not only to the Saddams and Assads but also to conservative Arab regimes, who are allies of the West.

9 March 1996

◆

Democracies, like human beings, have a tendency to relax when the worst is over.

10 December 1997

◆

America's duty is to lead: the other western countries' duty is to support its leadership.

10 December 1997

◆

Britain's reputation should be of vital importance to the Government of the day. Our reputation sustains our interests. The Pinochet case has sullied that reputation... This is a Pandora's box which has been opened – and unless Senator Pinochet returns safely to Chile, there will be no hope of closing it.

On the arrest of General Pinochet, 6 July 1999

◆

President Pinochet was this country's staunch, true friend in our time of need when Argentina seized the Falkland Islands. I know – I was Prime Minister at the time. On President Pinochet's express instructions, and at great risk, Chile provided enormously valuable assistance.

6 October 1999

◆

A new political alliance of the English-speaking peoples would allow us to foster those values that have been so important in our peace and prosperity and thus encourage that same peace and prosperity around the world.

Speech to the English Speaking Union, 7 December 1999

◆

Your detention in Britain was a great injustice which should never have taken place.

Letter to General Pinochet, 2000

◆

In many respects the challenge of Islamic terror is unique, hence the difficulty western intelligence services encountered trying to predict and prevent its onslaughts. The enemy is not, of course, a religion – most Muslims deplore what has occurred. Nor is it a single state, though this form of terrorism needs the support of states to give it succour. Perhaps the best parallel is with early Communism. Islamic extremism today, like Bolshevism in the past, is an armed doctrine. It is an aggressive ideology promoted by fanatical, well-armed devotees. And, like Communism, it requires an all-embracing long-term strategy to defeat it.

On Islamic terrorism, 11 February 2002

◆

America will never be the same again.

After the 9/11 attacks, 11 February 2002

◆

It is always exhilarating to visit New York. But nowadays it is also ennobling. This was the city which terrorists hated so much that they sought to tear out its very heart. But that heart still beats – proudly, strongly, passionately. Out of the ashes, from amid the tears, New Yorkers are once again rebuilding their City and their lives. Truly they are an inspiration to the world.

On the 9/11 attacks, 14 May 2003

◆

I am proud that Britain stood by America in this conflict. Our own Prime Minister was staunch; and our forces were superb. But, above all, it is President Bush who deserves the credit for victory. First in Afghanistan, and now in Iraq, the forces of tyranny and darkness have been routed. These victories have made our nations and our allies more secure. They have shown all who are tempted to do us harm that they will have to pay the price of their actions. Yes: the world remains dangerous. But it is yesterday's weakness, not today's resolve, which is to blame for the risks we face.

Speech to The Atlantic Bridge, 14 May 2003

◆

For years, many Governments played down the threats of Islamic revolution, turned a blind eye to international terrorism, and accepted the development of weaponry of mass destruction by dictators. Indeed, some politicians were happy to go further, collaborating with the self-proclaimed enemies of the West for their own short-term gain – but enough about the French!

14 May 2003

◆

We must not fall into the trap of projecting our own morality onto the Soviet leaders. They do not share our aspirations, they are not constrained by our ethics, they always consider themselves exempt from the rules that bind other states.

The Times, 30 September 1983

◆

Is there conscience in the Kremlin? Do they ever ask themselves what is the purpose of life? What is it all for? Their creed is barren of conscience, immune to the promptings of good and evil.

Speech at the Winston Churchill Foundation Dinner, 29 September 1983

◆

This heinous attack upon America was an attack upon us all. With America, Britain stands in the front line against Islamist fanatics who hate our beliefs, our liberties and our citizens. We must not falter. We must not fail.

On the fifth anniversary of the 9/11 attacks, 2006

◆

Evil, it is true, has always been with us. But evil was never so technically sophisticated, never so elusive, never so devoid of scruple, and never so anxious to inflict civilian casualties. The West must prevail – or else concede a reign of global lawlessness and violence unparalleled in modern times.

9 December 2002

◆

The claim that contrary to what appeared the case at the time, the Cold War wasn't really won, or if it was, it wasn't won by the Cold Warriors but in spite of them. Perhaps I should say 'in spite of us'. But the revisionists are wrong, and the Right was right.

Speech to the Hoover Institution, 19 July 2000

◆

In this twenty-first century the dominant power is America; the global language is English; the pervasive economic model is Anglo-Saxon capitalism – so why imprison ourselves in a bureaucratic Europe?

19 July 2000

♦

We know what works – the Anglo-Saxon model of liberty, property, law and capitalism. And we know where it works – everywhere it's actually applied. We must not be paralysed by false modesty or even good manners. Promoting the values that find their expression in America isn't imperialism, it's liberation.

19 July 2000

♦

I never hugged him. I bombed him.

On Colonel Gaddafi of Libya, 2011

ON THE FALKLANDS

Our judgement is that the presence of the Royal Marines garrison ... is sufficient deterrent against any possible aggression.

February 1982

◆

If they are invaded, we have got to get them back.

To Sir John Nott, 2 April 1982

◆

The people of the Falkland Islands, like the people of the United Kingdom, are an island race. They are few in number but they have the right to live in peace, to choose their own way of life and to determine their own allegiance. Their way of life is British; their allegiance is to the Crown. It is the wish of the British people and the duty of Her Majesty's Government to do everything that we can to uphold that right. That will be our hope and our endeavour, and, I believe, the resolve of every Member of this House.

In the House of Commons, 3 April 1982

◆

The Prime Minister, shortly after she came into office, received a sobriquet as the 'Iron Lady'. It arose in the context of remarks which she made about defence against the Soviet Union and its allies; but there was no reason to suppose that the Right Honourable Lady did not welcome and, indeed, take pride in that description. In the next week or two this House, the nation and the Right Honourable Lady herself, will learn of what metal she is made.

Enoch Powell, House of Commons, 3 April 1982

◆

I don't want to fight any wars; if you can get them off before we get there, you do it, but off they go.

To General Alexander Haig, 8 April 1982

◆

The British won't fight.

General Galtieri to Alexander Haig, 10 April 1982

◆

Ah, François, it's you. You are with me.

> To French President François Mitterrand, who had pledged his
> support in the Falklands conflict, April 1982

◆

When you stop a dictator there are always risks, but there are great risks in not stopping a dictator. My generation learnt that long ago.

> 1982

◆

I'm standing up for the right of self-determination. I'm standing up for our territory. I'm standing up for our people. I'm standing up for international law. I'm standing up for all those territories – those small territories and peoples the world over – who, if someone doesn't stand up and say to an invader 'enough, stop' ... would be at risk.

> *Panorama*, BBC TV, 26 April 1982

◆

It is exciting to have a real crisis on your hands, when you have spent half your political life dealing with humdrum issues like the environment.

> Scottish Conservative Party Conference, 14 May 1982

◆

Gentlemen, I have spent the night thinking about this Peruvian [peace] initiative and I have to tell you that if it is your decision to accept then you will have to find another Prime Minister.

To the War Cabinet, May 1982

◆

The Government wants a peaceful settlement. But we totally reject a peaceful sell-out.

Scottish Conservative Party Conference, 14 May 1982

◆

Just rejoice at that news and congratulate our armed forces and the Marines. Rejoice!

To journalists, following the retaking of South Georgia, May 1982

◆

Ron, I'm not handing over... I'm not handing over the islands now. I didn't lose some of my best ships and some of my finest lives to leave quietly under a ceasefire without the Argentines withdrawing.

To Ronald Reagan, 31 May 1982

◆

[Admiral] Lewin would come in and give the bad news straight away. He said he was sorry but the *Sheffield* had been sunk. That was one of the occasions when she would put her head down and stare at the table and I felt had really withdrawn herself from the War Cabinet, for about a minute. Then she'd shake herself and come back in again, tears running down her face.

Sir Michael Havers, *The Thatcher Factor*, Channel 4, 1990

◆

It shows that the substance under test consists of ferrous metal of the highest quality. It is of exceptional tensile strength, resistant to wear and tear, and may be used with advantage for all national purposes.

Enoch Powell explaining how the Iron Lady had stood up to the tests of the Falklands crisis

◆

We have ceased to be a nation in retreat. We have instead a newfound confidence – born in the economic battles at home and tested and found true 8,000 miles away... And so today, we can rejoice at our success in the Falklands and take pride in the achievement of the men and women of our task force. But we do so, not as some flickering of a flame which must soon be dead. No, we rejoice that Britain has rekindled that spirit which has fired her for generations past and which today has begun to burn as brightly as before. Britain found herself again in the South Atlantic and will not look back from the victory she has won.

3 July 1982

◆

You were thinking every moment of the day about it, it was at the back of your mind no matter what else you were doing. You were thinking of what was happening down there and the decisions that had to be taken. When the telephone went or one of the duty clerks came up with a piece of paper in his hand, you always braced yourself as the thought raced through your mind, 'is this bad news?' I never had any doubt about the Tightness of the decision. Even though we got the Task Forces there, there were voices saying, 'No, don't go and land, just negotiate'. I didn't go down there to negotiate. I went down there to get the Argentineans off and if they left then we didn't need to go into battle.

◆

The spirit of the South Atlantic was the spirit of Britain at her best. It has been said that we surprised the world, that British patriotism was rediscovered in those spring days. It was never really lost. But it would be no bad thing if the feeling that swept the country then were to continue to inspire us. For if there was any doubt about the determination of the British people it was removed by the men and women who, a few months ago, brought a renewed sense of pride and self-respect to our country.

Conservative Party Conference, 8 October 1982

♦

She was a decisive leader, which of course is what the military want. We don't want somebody who vacillates, we want to be able to put the case to her, the requirements to her, and say this is how it is, this is the decision we want, we want it now and we want it quickly and we don't want a wishy-washy decision, we want a clear-cut decision. She was magnificent in her support of the military.

Admiral Terry Lewin, Chief of the Defence Staff during the Falklands crisis

♦

Margaret Thatcher: Oh, arms to Argentina, you won't will you?
Ronald Reagan: No, we won't.

1987

♦

Twenty-five years ago British forces secured a great victory in a noble cause. The whole nation rejoiced at the success; and we should still rejoice. Aggression was defeated and reversed. The wishes of local people were upheld as paramount. Britain's honour and interests prevailed... Fortune does, in the end, favour the brave. And it is Britain's good fortune that none are braver than our armed forces. Thank you all.

Message on the twenty-fifth anniversary of the liberation of the Falklands, 13 June 2007

ON IRELAND

Northern Ireland is as British as Finchley.

◆

If you wash your hands of Northern Ireland you wash them in blood.

Conservative Party Conference, 13 October 1978

◆

Go back and tell everyone in the United States that this is what happens to the money they give to NORAID. Tell them not to send any more.

To two American tourists following the IRA bombing of the Chelsea Barracks, November 1979

◆

I think that was an assassination attempt, don't you?

To speechwriter Ronnie Millar a few minutes after the IRA
bomb went off in Brighton, 12 October 1984

◆

The bomb attack on the Grand Hotel early this morning
was first and foremost an inhuman, undiscriminating
attempt to massacre innocent, unsuspecting men and
women staying in Brighton for our Conservative Conference. Our first thoughts must at once be for those who
died and for those who are now in hospital recovering
from their injuries. But the bomb attack clearly signified
more than this. It was an attempt not only to disrupt and
terminate our conference; it was an attempt to cripple
Her Majesty's democratically elected Government. That
is the scale of the outrage we have all shared, and the fact
that we are gathered here now, shocked but composed and
determined, is a sign not only that this attack has failed
but that all attempts to destroy democracy by terrorism
will fail.

Conservative Party Conference, 12 October 1984

◆

In church on Sunday morning – it was lovely and we
haven't had many lovely days – the sun was coming
through the stained glass window and falling on some
flowers. It just occurred to me that this was the day I was

not meant to see. Then all of a sudden I thought 'there are some of my dearest friends who are not seeing this day'.

Following the IRA bomb attack on the Cabinet in Brighton, October 1984

◆

Now it must be business as usual.

Outside Brighton police station following the IRA bombing of the Grand Hotel, 1984

◆

I don't believe that the Prime Minister, when she said in 1979 'I'm a rock hard Unionist', was telling an untruth, I think she was correctly describing herself. She hated doing it. You only had to watch the Prime Minister in November 1985. She was a picture of misery. She just hated it. I suppose it is to her credit that having been convinced at that time that an overriding national interest was involved, she overrode her opinions, her wishes and her instincts.

Enoch Powell on the signing of the Anglo-Irish Agreement, *The Thatcher Factor*, Channel 4, 1990

◆

All of a sudden, the world is broken.

Following the IRA assassination of Ian Gow, August 1990

◆

It would be the equivalent of having the Prime Minister of England invite the Oklahoma City bombers to 10 Downing Street, to congratulate them on a job well done.

On President Clinton's welcome of Gerry Adams

◆

The people of Northern Ireland must not fall into the trap being set for them by the extremists. The cynical and evil men who lead the IRA want to goad outraged citizens to take the law into their own hands. There are those who might allow themselves to be provoked in this way: they must not give the IRA that satisfaction.

16 November 1981

◆

Be under no illusions about the Provisional IRA. They terrorise their own communities. They are the enemies of democracy and of freedom too. Don't just take my word for it. Ask the Government of the Irish Republic, where it is an offence even to belong to that organisation – as indeed it also is in Northern Ireland.

20 February 1985

◆

The Government will not falter in its search for a peaceful solution, but if the Protestant and Catholic communities choose to take arms against each other rather than to work together, the future will be dark. Revenge is no policy. Hatred gives birth only to hatred. Reconciliation is the path to peace and that is the path which this Government will continue to pursue.

16 November 1981

ON HER STYLE OF GOVERNMENT

We have made too much of one or two people, and we think that they can win or lose elections for us. Don't be depressed if one particular person transgresses. It doesn't lose an election unless the party loses faith in itself.

July 1963

◆

Power as a Minister doesn't give you power over the people. In the end, it's the people who have power over you.

Liverpool Daily Post, February 1972

◆

I don't want a Cabinet of yes-men or yes-women. It's not healthy. I can't stand sycophants.

1977

◆

There are two ways of making a Cabinet. One way is to have in it people representing the different points of view within the party, within the broad philosophy. The other way is to have in it only the people who want to go in the direction which every instinct tells me we have to go: clearly, steadily, firmly, with resolution. As Prime Minister, I could not waste my time having internal arguments.

1979

◆

I am not a consensus politician – I'm a conviction politician.

1977

◆

John Hoskyns [Head of Number 10 Policy Unit]: If there is ever to be any sort of U-turn on policy you absolutely must think about it now.
Margaret Thatcher: You know, I would rather go down than do that, so forget it.

1978

◆

I don't mind how much my Ministers talk, as long as they do what I say.

1980

♦

I love argument, I love debate. I don't expect anyone just to sit there and agree with me, that's not their job.

The Times, 1980

♦

The adrenalin flows when they really come out fighting at me, and I fight back and I stand there, and I know. Now come on Maggie, you are wholly on your own. No one can help you. And I love it!

1980

♦

If you have conviction people are much more likely to come out and support you. Most of the great faiths upon which our own moral values are founded would never have got started if their prophets had gone out to the people and said: 'Brothers, I believe in consensus.'

News of the World, September 1981

♦

I will not change just to court popularity. Indeed, if ever a Conservative Government start to do what they know to be wrong because they are afraid to do what they are sure is right, then is the time for Tories to cry 'Stop!' But you will never need to do that while I am Prime Minister.

Speech to the Conservative Party Conference, 16 October 1981

◆

I am painted as the greatest little dictator, which is ridiculous – you always take some consultations.

The Times, 1983

◆

We want as many Conservatives as we can possibly get. I think I could handle a landslide all right.

In response to Francis Pym's assertion that large majorities can be dangerous, June 1983

◆

I'm a tough boss, yes I drive people, but it's my job to do that. But it's utterly ridiculous to call me a dictator.

1984

◆

We got a really good consensus during the last election. Consensus behind my convictions.

1984

◆

What is this thing called consensus? Consensus is something you reach when you cannot agree.

◆

I go for agreement – agreement for the things I want to do.

The Times, 10 April 1984

◆

I don't spend a lifetime watching which way the cat jumps. I know really which way I want the cats to go.

1985

◆

Obviously at sometime or other you have to hand over to someone new, fresh, young, dynamic. You do not want to cling on so they have to say: 'Who is going to tell the old girl she had better go?'

1985

◆

I am the Cabinet rebel.

◆

We believe a Government's task is to give people the opportunity, not a handout.

◆

Well I don't know why we are meeting. It is quite clear this matter must be settled and in fact I thought it was. So shall we just check some of the details?

As attributed to her by Kenneth Baker

◆

I don't believe they [the voters] want a Government to be so flexible it becomes invertebrate. You don't want a Government full of flexi-toys.

1985

◆

I sent them there to support me. They ought to know better.

On Conservative peers who voted against the Government

◆

Margaret Thatcher: You will make no further statements or answer questions. This is the decision of the Cabinet and I must ask you to accept it.

Michael Heseltine: I cannot hesitate in supporting what I have said. There has been a breakdown of collective responsibility and I must therefore leave the Cabinet.

9 January 1986

♦

We have a style of great discussion and great debate. That has always been characteristic of my handling of Government.

To American journalists, 18 January 1986

♦

This is only the third time of asking. I hope to go on and on and on.

During the general election campaign, May 1987

♦

I am staying my own sweet, reasonable self.

Following the resignation of Nigel Lawson, October 1989

♦

You get a long way by nagging – nobody argued with me.

After the Dublin EC summit, March 1990

◆

I think sometimes the Prime Minister should be intimidating. There's not much point being a weak, floppy thing in the chair, is there?

1993

◆

I do not believe that collective responsibility is an interesting fiction, but a point of principle.

The Downing Street Years, 1993

◆

I hated sacking Ministers and I could not prevent myself thinking what it meant to them and their families, suddenly losing salary, car and prestige.

The Downing Street Years, 1993

ON THE ECONOMY

We should not underestimate the enormity of the task which lies ahead. But little can be achieved without sound money. It is the bedrock of sound government.

May 1979

◆

Oh that Gilbert and Sullivan should be living in this hour. This [the Selective Employment Tax] is sheer cockeyed lunacy. The Chancellor needs a woman at the Treasury.

March 1966

◆

It costs just as much to train a bad teacher as it does to train a good teacher.

1973

◆

I do not believe it is in the character of the British people to begrudge the lion's share to those who have genuinely played the lion's part. They are ready to recognise that those who create the wealth – and I mean not only material but intellectual wealth – enrich the whole nation.

London Evening News, September 1974

◆

Never in the history of human credit has so much been owed.

1975

◆

Free enterprise has enabled the creative and the acquisitive urges of man to be given expression in a way which benefits all members of society. Let free enterprise light back now, not for itself, but for all those who believe in freedom.

July 1975

◆

There are too few rich and too few profits.

1984

◆

We have rising prosperity and rising generosity at home. We see a rising spirit of cooperation in the world. We can be optimistic about the future, but one thing is sure: there will be just as many challenges and just as many opportunities ahead of us. History will not do our work for us. The future is in our own hands. It will be up to free men and women to surmount the challenges and grasp the opportunities. I believe they will and that the years ahead will be great ones for this country.

Lord Mayor's Banquet, 1988

◆

When you take into public ownership a profitable industry the profits soon disappear. The goose that laid the golden eggs goes broody. State geese are not great layers.

◆

Our aim is to make tax collecting a declining industry.

Conservative Party Conference, 14 October 1977

◆

Any woman who understands the problems of running a home will be near to understanding the problems of running a nation.

The Observer, 8 May 1979

◆

It is economic liberty that nourishes the enterprise of those whose hard work and imagination ultimately determine the conditions in which we live. It is economic liberty that makes possible a free press. It is economic liberty that has enabled the modern democratic state to provide a decent minimum of welfare for the citizen, while leaving him free to choose when, where, and how he will make his own contribution to the economic life of the country. If the economic life of the country is dominated by the state, few of these things, are true.

Winston Churchill Memorial Lecture, 18 October 1979

◆

We need to create a mood where it is everywhere thought morally right for as many people as possible to acquire capital.

July 1979

◆

Nothing is beyond this nation. Decline is not inevitable. They say I'm an optimist. Well, in this job you get called all sorts of things. An optimist is one of the nicer ones and I would not deny the label. I remember what our country used to be like and I know what we can become again. But first we must rid ourselves of the idea that the laws of economic gravity can somehow be suspended in our favour and that what applies to other nations does not apply to ours.

16 October 1981

◆

It is your tax which pays for public spending. The Government have no money of their own. There is only taxpayers' money.

Conservative Party Conference, 12 October 1979

◆

Pennies don't fall from heaven, they have to be earned on earth.

Sunday Telegraph, November 1979

◆

We shall take whatever action is necessary to contain the growth of the money supply. The Government, unlike so many of its predecessors, will face up to economic realities.

Speech to the Lord Mayor's Banquet, November 1979

◆

We should not expect the state to appear in the guise of an extravagant good fairy at every christening, a loquacious companion at every stage of life's journey, the unknown mourner at every funeral.

March 1980

◆

Inflation is the cause of unemployment, not an alternative to it.

◆

I will have to say to all public utilities, 'look, if you are just demanding something for nothing, you're demanding it from your fellow citizens and they too will have something to say about that,' but this all the time is trying to get across to people, and it's part of what you would call 'The Thatcher Experiment'. There isn't a pot of gold to draw on, there is either your own extra effort, working machinery better, or you're taking something from your fellow citizens.

Interview with Brian Walden, 1979

◆

As well as a right to strike, there is a right to work. As well as the justice of a demand, there is the injustice that industrial action may inflict on others. As well as a loyalty to the union, there is a loyalty to family and to company. As well as a right to a decent wage, there is a duty to society to provide essential services. It had become abundantly clear that, just as the unions had at one time sought redress from the arbitrary actions of employers, so today individuals, businesses and citizens were seeking protection from the power and might of trade unions.

House of Commons, 28 February 1980

◆

Trade has been a great engine of post-war growth. All have gained from the greater freedom of trade and payments. Freer trade has meant lower prices, more competition and faster growth. And every consumer has benefited.

16 November 1981

◆

What then is the lesson of the post-war success and of the hard changes of the 1970s? The lesson must be that it would be the utmost folly if, at this crucial time, we turned away from the freedom which has served the most successful countries of the world so well and for so long. That way would impoverish the British people.

Lord Mayor's Banquet, 16 November 1981

◆

Bills have to be paid.

16 November 1981

◆

We do not measure our success merely by how much money the Government spends. The well-being of our people is about far more than the welfare state. It is about self-reliance, family help, voluntary help as well as state provision. In a society which is truly healthy responsibility is shared and help is mutual. Wherever we can we shall extend the opportunity for personal ownership and the self-respect that goes with it.

8 October 1982

♦

We have to get our production and our earnings in balance. There's no easy popularity in what we are proposing, but it is fundamentally sound. Yet I believe people accept there is no real alternative.

Conservative Women's Conference, 22 May 1980

♦

What really gets me is this – it's very ironic that those who are most critical of extra tax are those who are most vociferous in demanding extra expenditure. What gets me even more is that having demanded that extra expenditure they are not prepared to face the consequences of their own action and stand by the necessity to get the tax to pay for it. I wish some of them had a bit more guts and courage than they have.

Referring to the Tory 'wets', 1981

♦

Economics are the method. The object is to change the heart and soul.

Sunday Times, 3 May 1981

◆

Inflation can and must be defeated, and defeated for good.

◆

The secret of happiness is to live within your income and pay your bills on time.

◆

A quick cure is a quack cure.

On unemployment, 27 May 1983

◆

I don't agree with you. You start off by saying there is more hope than certainty. There is no certainty in this world. There is not. I was born and bred in business. Are you telling me there is any certainty in next year's income? If you are doing well, you're worried about the future when you might not be doing so well. If you're not doing well, it's a fight to get more business. There is no certainty. I don't know what the people of Britain will choose to buy next year. I don't suppose a housewife knows what she'll choose to buy next year. I don't suppose a worker who's wanting to buy a car will know which car he's going to buy next year – he won't know the designs that are available. I don't know what will happen in the Middle East. After all, the wars and the politics there caused the first world recession. I don't know what'll happen to interest rates in the rest of the world. To try to convey the impression that we live in a world which is fixed and certain is totally and utterly wrong.

Interview with Brian Walden, 5 June 1983

◆

The Winter of Discontent had shocked us all. Britain's defences had been undermined. The police were demoralised. All too plainly we were a nation which had lost its way. And we were on the brink of the deepest recession since the 1930s. It was a bleak inheritence, perhaps the bleakest any newly elected British Government had faced since the War. But you elected us to face it, and face it we did, squarely. No fudging. No dodging. No muddling along. No making do with second best, because second best so quickly turns into third best, and third best into a downward spiral of decline. This Government was determined to restore Britain's health and Britain's pride. To halt the decline left by Labour. To revive our economy. To lift the nation and reawaken its spirit.

Speech to the Welsh Conservatives, 1983

◆

Government after Government has learnt the same lesson – or should have. Labour's Manifesto reminds us that some people never learn. The lesson is simple – runaway inflation runs away with your most cherished plans – not to mention your savings.

◆

You can't buck the market.

On Chancellor Nigel Lawson's attempts to shadow the Deutsche
Mark, 1989

◆

Governments should not run business.

10 December 1986

◆

Popular capitalism is nothing less than a crusade to
enfranchise the many in the economic life of the nation.
We Conservatives are returning power to the people.
That is the way to one nation, one people.

Conservative Party Conference, 10 October 1986

◆

Sanctions only work by causing unemployment and starvation and misery. And the people who regard themselves
as civilised and compassionate should proceed by wanting to increase unemployment in a country where there
is no social security, poverty, hunger and starvation, then
I do not think very much to their sincerity and I think
that they should take a different view.

On economic sanctions, 21 February 1990

◆

I do wish I had brought my cheque book. I don't believe in credit cards.

At the Ideal Home Exhibition, March 1990

◆

I don't believe you can go on spending money you haven't got.

◆

We exploded the myth that Governments can spend their way to economic revival – a half doctrine of Maynard Keynes peddled by those who persistently ignore the other half.

14 November 1983

◆

The most debilitating myth was that the state can perpetually provide a higher standard of living regardless of individual effort. It can't and it never could.

14 November 1983

◆

You may remember in 1981 when Sir Geoffrey Howe took his courageous steps to cut Government borrowing,

364 economists united in condemning his action. 364 economists one for almost every day of the year. What an alarming thought. And all of them actually in agreement! They said the Chancellor was wrong. They said he would deepen the recession. It was they who were wrong for Britain's recovery dates from that time.

Lord Mayor's Banquet, 1983

♦

Why are we Conservatives so opposed to inflation? Only because it puts up prices? No, because it destroys the value of people's savings. Because it destroys jobs, and with it people's hopes. That's what the fight against inflation is all about.

Why have we limited the power of trade unions? Only to improve productivity? No, because trade union members, want to be protected from intimidation and to go about their daily lives in peace – like everyone else in the land.

Why have we allowed people to buy shares in nationalised industries? Only to improve efficiency? No. To spread the nation's wealth among as many people as possible.

Why are we setting up new kinds of schools in our towns and cities? To create privilege? No. To give families in some of our inner cities greater choice in the education of their children.

Conservative Party Conference, 1986

♦

That is what capitalism is: a system that brings wealth to many, not just to the few.

Speech to the Joint Meeting of US Congress, 20 February 1985

◆

Interviewer: That is a fairness point Labour thinks that they have got and you have not got about the distribution of wealth, their argument is the rich get richer and the poor get poorer.

Prime Minister: That is nonsense, that is absolute nonsense, we have got a wider distribution of wealth than we have ever had before. In England 68 per cent of people own their own homes. It was 11 million when we came into power and it is now 15 million. One in five own their own shares. There are something like 17 million savers on building societies. And, is it not very interesting, that these days if you have your house plus anything less than £8,000 in savings, you rank for social security? That is a new definition, is it not?

Interview for the *Sunday Times*, 21 February 1990

◆

It is ironic that we should be accused of wanting unemployment to solve our economic problems by the very Government which has produced record post-war unemployment, and is expecting more.

Speech to the Conservative Party Conference, 10 October 1975

◆

Unemployment may be an unpalatable consequence of fighting inflation.

Sunday Times, 3 August 1980

◆

We Conservatives hate unemployment. We hate the idea of men and women not being able to use their abilities. We deplore the waste of national resources and the deep affront to people's dignity by being out of work through no fault of their own.

Speech to the Conservative Party Conference, 10 October 1975

◆

I think it's terrible if a person who wants to work cannot find a job. You have no self-respect, you haven't got the respect of your family, if somehow you cannot earn yourself a living and them a living too.

Party political broadcast, 4 May 1977

◆

Britain is one of the few countries creating jobs.

House of Commons, 8 May 1985

◆

The number of people in work had increased by 700,000 since October 1983... Yes, many of the jobs have been part-time, and what is wrong with that?

House of Commons, 30 January 1986

◆

Everything a politician promises at election time has to be paid for either by higher taxation or by borrowing.

28 March 1992

◆

The trade cycle is a permanent fact of economic life, which politicians can ameliorate by sensible policies, or aggravate by foolish ones, but which they can't abolish altogether.

Speech to the Economic Club of New York, 18 June 1991

◆

Economic freedom is real freedom. Just as coercion exercised on economic grounds is no less real coercion.

4 October 1994

◆

Governments do not create the wealth. They consume it. It is the people who create the wealth and they need the incentive of tax cuts to do it.

28 April 1988

ON EUROPE

Naturally, it is with some temerity that the pupil speaks before the master, because you know more about the Common Market than anybody.

To Edward Heath at a Keep Britain in Europe meeting, 1975 –
Mr Heath ignored her

◆

I believe we should continue to have a partnership of national states each retaining the right to protect its vital interests, but developing more effectively than at present the habit of working together.

Conservative Party Campaign Guide, 1977

◆

It has been suggested by some people in this country that I and my Government will be a 'soft touch' in the Community. In case such a rumour may have reached your ears, Mr Chancellor ... it is only fair to advise you frankly to dismiss it, as my colleagues did long ago! I intend to be very discriminating in judging what are British interests and I shall be resolute in defending them.

Speech at a dinner in honour of German Chancellor Helmut Schmidt, May 1979

◆

We believe in a free Europe, not a standardised Europe. Diminish that variety within the member states, and you impoverish the whole Community. We insist that the institutions of the European Community are managed so that they increase the liberty of the individual throughout the Continent. These institutions must not be permitted to dwindle into bureaucracy. Whenever they fail to enlarge freedom the institutions should be criticised and the balance restored.

July 1979

◆

I have the money and they won't get their hands on it.

To Sir Nicholas Henderson, referring to Britain's EC budget contributions, 13 August 1979

◆

They are all a rotten lot. Schmidt and the Americans and we are the only people who would do any standing up and fighting if necessary.

On fellow European leaders, 1979

◆

I must be absolutely clear about this. Britain cannot accept the present situation on the budget. It is demonstrably unjust. It is politically indefensible. I cannot play Sister Bountiful to the Community while my own electorate are being asked to forgo improvements in the fields of health, education, welfare and the rest.

Winston Churchill Memorial Lecture, Luxembourg, 18 October 1980

◆

I want my money back!

Dublin EC summit, November 1980

◆

[On other EEC heads of state] I can cope with nine of them, so they ought to be able to stand one of me. They could end the tiresomeness and stubbornness by giving me what I want.

The Times, 10 April 1984

◆

Mr Chairman, you have invited me to speak on the subject of Britain and Europe. Perhaps I should congratulate you on your courage. If you believe some of the things said and written about my views on Europe, it must seem rather like inviting Genghis Khan to speak on the virtues of peaceful co-existence.

Speech to the College of Europe, Bruges, 20 September 1988

◆

My first guiding principle is this: willing and active cooperation between independent sovereign states... Europe will be stronger precisely because it has France as France, Spain as Spain, Britain as Britain, each with its own customs, traditions and identity. It would be folly to try to fit them into some sort of identikit European personality.

Speech to the College of Europe, Bruges, 20 September 1988

◆

We have not successfully rolled back the frontiers of the state in Britain, only to see them re-imposed at a European level, with a European Super-State exercising a new dominance from Brussels.

Speech to the College of Europe, Bruges, 20 September 1988

◆

When the time is right.

The mantra for joining the European Exchange Rate Mechanism

◆

To go to a single currency is not just a practical matter: it is a fundamental question of principle. It is not only a merger of currencies: it is to give up for all time the right of the Banks of England and of Scotland and our Treasury to issue our own currency, backed by our own economic policy, answerable to our own Parliament. That is why I do not believe in a single currency.

House of Commons, 26 January 1991

◆

Human rights did not begin with the French Revolution ... [they] really stem from a mixture of Judaism and Christianity ... [we English] had 1688, our quiet revolution, where Parliament exerted its will over the King... It was not the sort of revolution that France's was ... 'liberty, equality, fraternity' – they forgot obligations and duties I think. And then, of course the fraternity went missing for a long time.

Interview with *Le Monde*, 1989

◆

It took us a long time to get rid of the effects of the French Revolution 200 years ago. We don't want another one.

30 June 1989

◆

Broadly speaking, for every £2 we contribute we get £1 back. That leaves us with a net contribution of £1,000 million pounds next year to the Community and rising in the future. It is that £1,000 million on which we started to negotiate, because we want the greater part back. But it is not asking the Community for money; it is asking the Community to have our own money back, and I frequently said to them: 'Look! We, as one of the poorer members of the Community, cannot go on filling the coffers of the Community. We are giving you notice that we just cannot afford it!'

Press Conference after the Dublin European Council, 30 November 1979

◆

To accuse Mrs Thatcher of wishing to torpedo Europe because she defends the interests of her country with great determination is to question her underlying intentions in the same way that people used to question those of de Gaulle in regard to French interests.

Le Figaro, November 1990

◆

It seems like cloud cuckoo land... If anyone is suggesting that I would go to Parliament and suggest the abolition of the Pound Sterling – no!... We have made it quite clear that we will not have a single currency imposed upon us.

October 1990

◆

Yes, the Commission wants to increase its powers. Yes, it is a non-elected body and I do not want the Commission to increase its powers at the expense of the House, so of course we differ. The President of the Commission, Mr Delors, said at a press conference the other day that he wanted the European Parliament to be the democratic body of the Community. He wanted the Commission to be the Executive and he wanted the Council of Ministers to be the Senate. No! No! No!

Hansard, 30 October 1990

◆

All part of my vision of a wider Europe.

On the fall of the Berlin Wall, November 1990

◆

Our entry into the ERM has been warmly welcomed by our Community partners. But as John Major made absolutely clear yesterday, this Government has no intention of agreeing to the imposition of a single currency.

That would be entering a federal Europe through the back-Delors.

Conservative Party Conference, 1990

◆

A democratic Europe of nation states could be a force for liberty, enterprise and open trade. But, if creating a United States of Europe overrides these goals, the new Europe will be one of subsidy and protection.

Speech to the American Conservative Institutes, 8 March 1991

◆

When will Labour learn that you cannot build Jerusalem in Brussels.

1992

◆

If I were a German today, I would be proud, proud but also worried. I would be proud of the magnificent achievement of rebuilding my country, entrenching democracy and assuming the undoubtedly preponderant position in Europe. But a united Germany can't and won't subordinate its national interests in economic or in foreign policy to those of the Community indefinitely. Germany's new pre-eminence is a fact ... and its power is a problem – as much for Germans as for the rest of Europe.

15 May 1992

◆

I pay tribute to John Major's achievement in persuading the other eleven Community heads of Government that they could move ahead to the Social Chapter but not within the Treaty and without Britain's participation. It sets a vital precedent, for an enlarged Community can only function if we build in flexibility of that kind. John Major deserves high praise for ensuring at Maastricht that we would not have either a single currency or the absurd provisions of the Social Chapter forced upon us: our industry, workforce and national prosperity will benefit as a result.

15 May 1992

◆

We weren't getting a fair deal on the budget and I wasn't going to have it. There's a great strand of equity and fairness in the British people – this is our characteristic. There's not a strand of equity and fairness in Europe.

They're out to get as much as they can. That's one of those enormous differences. So I tackled it on that basis.

BBC TV, 1993

◆

If there is one instance in which a foreign policy I pursued met with unambiguous failure, it was my policy on German reunification.

The Downing Street Years, 1993

◆

I had the effect of cementing the Anglo-American alliance. What's the good of having bases if when you want to use them you're not allowed to by the home country. It made America realise that Britain was her real and true friend, when they were hard up against it and wanted something, and that no one else in Europe was. They're a weak lot, some of them in Europe you know. Weak. Feeble.

On the American air strike on Libya, BBC TV, 1993

◆

We have been a little like an accomplice in a massacre. We cannot carry on like that.

On the West's role in Bosnia, 17 April 1993

◆

The lesson of this century is that Europe will only be peaceful if the Americans are on this continent.

18 April 1993

◆

In my day that would have required the occasional use of the handbag. Now it will be a cricket bat. But that's a good thing because it will be harder.

On John Major's negotiations on the Maastricht Treaty, 1993

◆

I personally could never have signed this Treaty.

On the Maastricht Treaty, 12 June 1993

◆

It is the people's turn to speak. It is their powers of which we are the custodians.

Calling for a referendum on the Maastricht Treaty, 17 July 1993

◆

If Margaret Thatcher had been Prime Minister at the time, there would have been no Treaty of Maastricht.

Douglas Hurd, 6 November 1993

◆

I was turned out because I said to Europe no, no, no. That no, no, no has now turned into yes, yes. Two yes's not three because he got the Social Chapter out and he's reserved his position on the single currency.

Interview with Sir David Frost, 1994

◆

My friends, we are quite the best country in Europe. I've been told I have to be careful about what I say and I don't like it. In my lifetime all our problems have come from

mainland Europe and all the solutions have come from
the English-speaking nations across the world.

Speech to Scottish Tories, 1999

◆

To surrender the pound, to surrender our power of self-
government, would betray all that past generations down
the ages lived and died to defend.

22 May 2001

◆

'Europe' in anything other than the geographical sense
is a wholly artificial construct. It makes no sense at all
to lump together Beethoven and Debussy, Voltaire and
Burke, Vermeer and Picasso, Notre Dame and St Paul's,
boiled beef and bouillabaisse, and portray them as
elements of a 'European' musical, philosophical, artistic,
architectural or gastronomic reality. If Europe charms
us, as it has so often charmed me, it is precisely because
of its contrasts and contradictions, not its coherence and
continuity.

Statecraft, 2003

◆

What we should grasp, however, from the lessons of
European history is that, first, there is nothing necessarily
benevolent about programmes of European integration;

second, the desire to achieve grand utopian plans often poses a grave threat to freedom; and third, European unity has been tried before, and the outcome was far from happy.

Statecraft, 2003

◆

I wholeheartedly support *The Sun*'s campaign for a referendum on the new EU treaty.

Yet again the British people are being told that the changes in the Treaty are not important, that they are technical, and that in any case we have either blocked or gained opt-outs in all the worst cases.

Well, we've heard it all before only to see more and more powers grabbed by Brussels.

So yet again *Sun* readers are standing up for Britain and calling our Government to account.

This Treaty is a blueprint for a European Constitution in all but name a Constitution which has already been rejected.

But that's one little 'technicality' the Brussels bureaucrats want us to forget.

So may I say to the Prime Minister, don't believe the assurances from Brussels, they gave similar ones to me!

It's not too late to listen and it's not too late to act.

This Treaty matters Prime Minister, so be bold and let the British people have the final say!

The Sun, 29 September 2007

ON CONSERVATIVES

I'll always be fond of dear Ted, but there's no sympathy in politics.

On former Prime Minister Edward Heath, 1975

◆

They broke Keith, but they won't break me.

On Sir Keith Joseph, January 1975

◆

When I look at him [Edward Heath] and he looks at me, I don't feel that it is a man looking at a woman. More like a woman being looked at by another woman.

To Sir John Junor, 1979

◆

We all make mistakes now and then. I think it was a mistake, and Jim Prior was very, very sorry indeed for it, and very apologetic. But you don't just sack a chap for one mistake.

On Jim Prior, following his criticism of the British Steel management, 21 January 1980

◆

I got the distinct impression that he felt he was being dismissed by his housemaid.

On the dismissal of Christopher Soames from her Cabinet, 1981

◆

The trouble with you is you talk too much. You remind me of Robert Carr.

On Kenneth Clarke [as reported by Kenneth Baker]

◆

Keith and I have no toes.

On Sir Keith Joseph

◆

The greatest team player in British politics, a straight bat at the wicket, steady on the green, mighty in the scrum.

On Willie Whitelaw

◆

Douglas, Douglas, you would make Neville Chamberlain look like a warmonger.

On Douglas Hurd

◆

He supported me steadfastly when I was right, and, more important, when I wasn't.

On Willie Whitelaw, *The Downing Street Years*, 1993

◆

Others bring me problems, David brings me solutions.

On David [later Lord] Young, 1990

◆

He thinks in paragraphs.

On Lord Cockfield

◆

The trouble with Nigel is that he's a gambler.

On Nigel Lawson

◆

He has given this country great service. He is the only one who really thinks the same way as I do.

On Cecil Parkinson, 9 April 1986

◆

The thing about us, Bernard, is that neither of us are smooth people.

To Sir Bernard Ingham

◆

I was told that Bernard's politics had been Labour, not Conservative; but the first time we met I warmed to this tough, blunt, humorous Yorkshireman. Bernard's outstanding virtue was his total integrity. An honest man himself, he expected the same high standards from others. He never let me down.

The Downing Street Years, 1993

◆

My Foreign Secretary said if I didn't commit myself to a date, he'd resign. Well I didn't commit myself, and he hasn't resigned. What sort of Foreign Secretary have I got?

Sir Geoffrey Howe after the Madrid summit, referring to a commitment to join the Exchange Rate Mechanism, July 1989

◆

He is another one of us.

On John Major, 1989

◆

John Gummer just did not have the political clout or credibility to rally the troops. I had appointed him as a sort of nightwatchman, but he seemed to have to sleep on the job.

On John Gummer's period as Chairman of the Conservative Party, *The Downing Street Years*, 1993

◆

He was the extrovert's extrovert. He had prodigious energy; he was and remains the most popular speaker the party has ever had... Unfortunately, as it turned out, Jeffrey's political judgement did not always match his enormous energy and fund-raising ability: ill-considered remarks got him and the party into somewhat awkward scrapes, but he always got himself out of them.

On Jeffrey Archer, *The Downing Street Years*, 1993

◆

Geoffrey was regularly bullied in debate by Denis Healey. But by thorough mastery of his brief and an ability to marshal arguments and advice from different sources, he had shown that beneath a deceptively mild exterior he had the makings of the fine Chancellor he was to become. Some of the toughest decisions were to fall to him. He never flinched. In my view, these were his best political years.

On Sir Geoffrey Howe, *The Downing Street Years*, 1993

◆

Nigel was secretive. I think he was a man of many complexes, he was also a man of many, many talents, sometimes a very creative person will also have great drawbacks. He did some very imaginative Budgets in income tax. He wrote the best Budgets as far as style is concerned that we've ever had. I always took the view that you had to take the rough with the smooth. If you have someone with great talent and ability you have to take some of the drawbacks too.

On Nigel Lawson, BBC TV, 1993

◆

He was never popular with the general public who saw what appeared to be a chain-smoking, dishevelled, languid aristocrat; by contrast, he was the object of universal respect and great affection from those who worked with him, above all his officials. Nick had those virtues which seem only to be cultivated in private: he was completely unaffected; he treated people and arguments on their merits; he was incapable of guile; and he was always seeking to take on the unrewarding and unpopular tasks.

On Nicholas Ridley, *The Downing Street Years*, 1993

◆

Geoffrey's personal style was very different from mine. He has a lovely speaking voice, a quiet speaking voice. But at Cabinet he always reported on foreign affairs – he always had this quiet voice. It was so quiet sometimes I had to say 'speak up'. And he gave it in a way which wasn't exactly scintillating. And you know, foreign affairs are interesting. They affect everything that happened to our own way of life, and they are exciting. And so we just diverged.

On Sir Geoffrey Howe, BBC TV, 1993

◆

I will not take any criticism of Bernard. I could wish that every one of my Ministers had done their job to the same percentage of excellence that Bernard did his.

On Sir Bernard Ingham, BBC TV, 1993

◆

John is much more a consensus man, and will much more compromise. I had noticed that he tended to go with the crowd and the conventional wisdom, but therefore he needed to be tested to see how he would perform in other roles... People like John very much, you couldn't not like him. But it's quite different from liking a person, to having a political instinct of the right direction to go in the long run. Perhaps I had developed that over the years.

On John Major, BBC TV, 1993

◆

Today I have lost one of my dearest friends, England one of her greatest men. Keith Joseph understood that it was necessary to win again the intellectual argument for freedom, and that to do this we must start from first principles... He was in many ways an unlikely revolutionary. For all his towering intellect, he was deeply humble. He spoke out boldly, however hostile the audience. Yet he hated to give offence. Above all, his integrity shone out in everything he said and did. His best memorial lies in the younger generations of politicians whom he inspired. But for me he is irreplaceable.

Tribute to Lord Joseph on the day he died, 10 December 1994

◆

Ted Heath was a political giant. He was also, in every sense, the first modern Conservative leader – by his humble background, his grammar school education and by the fact of his democratic election. As Prime Minister, he was confronted by the enormous problems of post-war Britain. If those problems eventually defeated him, he had shown in the 1970 manifesto how they, in turn, would eventually be defeated. For that, and much else besides, we are all in his debt.

On the death of Edward Heath, 2005

◆

Milton Friedman revived the economics of liberty when it had been all but forgotten. He was an intellectual freedom fighter. Never was there a less dismal practitioner of a dismal science. I shall greatly miss my old friend's lucid wisdom and mordant humour.

On the death of Milton Friedman, 2006

◆

Bill was a dear friend who will be greatly missed. He had a uniquely distinguished career in politics and journalism. He managed to appeal to new generations just as effectively as he did to earlier ones. I am deeply sorry at his passing.

On the death of Bill Deedes, 2007

◆

I simply do not understand how Ken could lead today's Conservative Party to anything other than disaster.

On Ken Clarke, 2001

◆

He is a remarkable politician, quite a remarkable person, a fantastic brain.

On Enoch Powell

ON HER POLITICAL OPPONENTS

A very good talker, but he is not a doer.

On Harold Wilson, February 1966

◆

Some Chancellors are micro-economic, are fiscal. This one is just plain cheap... If this Chancellor can be Chancellor, anyone in the House could be Chancellor.

On Denis Healey, January 1975

◆

Tony Benn is a skilful politician. He knows when to keep quiet.

1979

◆

He presided over debt, drift and decay.

On James Callaghan

◆

The SDP MPs should have stayed within the Labour Party and fought from within it. But they hadn't got the guts.

1 June 1983

◆

You would think that his wife would advise him better wouldn't you?

On Michael Foot's dress sense, following the Cenotaph service where he wore a donkey jacket

◆

I could not help feeling sorry for James Callaghan, who just a little bit earlier had conceded victory in a short speech, both dignified and generous. Whatever our past and indeed future disagreements, I believed him to be a patriot with the interests of Britain at heart, whose worst tribulations had been inflicted by his own party.

The Downing Street Years, 1993

◆

The marriage is for one election only. After that either party can call it a day and go its separate way. Well, of course, nothing is for ever. But it is an odd couple that pencils in a date for divorce before they have even sat down to the wedding breakfast.

On the SDP–Liberal Alliance, Conservative Party Conference, 16 October 1981

◆

You belong to the North East, why don't you boost it? Not always standing there as moaning minnies. Now stop it!

Description of journalists on Tyneside

◆

You don't reach Downing Street by pretending you've travelled the road to Damascus when you haven't even left home.

On Neil Kinnock, 1989

◆

Little Sir Echo.

On Neil Kinnock, January 1985

◆

As for the leaders of the former Alliance parties, I will say no more than this: they have never learnt what every woman knows – that you can't make a soufflé rise twice.

Conservative Party Conference, 13 October 1989

◆

Leading the Labour Party in opposition must be a nightmare. But I found it difficult to sympathise with Neil Kinnock. He was involved in what seemed to me a fundamentally discreditable enterprise, that of making himself and his party appear what they were not. The House of Commons and the electorate found him out. As Opposition leader he was out of his depth. As Prime Minister he would have been sunk.

On Neil Kinnock, *The Downing Street Years*, 1993

◆

He is probably the most formidable leader we have seen since Gaitskell. I see a lot of Socialism behind their front bench but not in Mr Blair – I think he genuinely has moved.

On Tony Blair, BBC TV, 1994

◆

I was very sorry to hear the news. He was a great parliamentarian and a man of high principles.

On the death of Michael Foot

◆

Jim Callaghan was a formidable opponent, one who could best me across the despatch box. In other circumstances he would have been a successful Prime Minister. He was a superb party manager. Despite our disagreements, I always respected him because I knew he was moved by deep patriotism.

On the death of Jim Callaghan, 2005

ON FOREIGN LEADERS

He may be a Socialist, but his economic views are more sensible than those of the wets.

On Helmut Schmidt, November 1979

◆

It was impossible not to like Jimmy Carter. He was a deeply committed Christian and a man of obvious sincerity. He was also a man of marked intellectual ability and with a grasp, rare among politicians, of science and the scientific method.

On President Carter, *The Downing Street Years*, 1993

◆

Charles Haughey was tough, able and politically astute with few illusions and, I am sure, not much affection for the British... I found him easy to get on with, less talkative and more realistic than Garret Fitzgerald.

The Downing Street Years, 1993

◆

President Giscard d'Estaing was never someone to whom I warmed. I had the strong impression that the feeling was mutual. This was more surprising than it seems, for I have a soft spot for French charm and, after all, President Giscard was seen as a man of the Right. But he was a difficult interlocutor, speaking in paragraphs of perfectly crafted prose which seemed to brook no interruption.

On President Giscard d'Estaing, *The Downing Street Years*, 1993

◆

He seemed to have a positive aversion to principle, even a conviction that a man of principle was doomed to be a figure of fun.

On Giulio Andreotti, *The Downing Street Years*, 1993

◆

Pierre, you're being obnoxious. Stop acting like a naughty schoolboy.

On Pierre Trudeau, 1981

◆

The election of a man [Ronald Reagan] committed to the cause of freedom and the renewal of America's strength has given encouragement to all those who love liberty.

February 1981

◆

I liked and respected Indira Gandhi. Her policies had been more than high-handed, but only a strong figure with a powerful personality could hope successfully to rule India. Mrs Gandhi was also, perhaps it is not just myth to see this as a female trait – immensely practical. Her weak spot was that she never grasped the importance of the free market.

The Downing Street Years, 1993

◆

I support very much the approaches that the President is taking. As you know, I am his greatest fan.

On Ronald Reagan, *The Times*, 18 February 1985

◆

It's a pity about Ronnie [Reagan], he just doesn't understand economics at all.

1983

◆

We were a threesome, and I hope that together we managed to do quite a lot for peace and democracy.

On Mikhail Gorbachev and Ronald Reagan

◆

Helmut Schmidt sent nearly half a million *Gastarbeiter* [immigrant workers] home, which we couldn't do, and he's got compulsory conscription which takes a whole year of young people off the unemployment register. So yes, I get on extremely well with Helmut Schmidt. My policies and his were the same.

BBC Radio, March 1983

◆

I like Mr Gorbachev. We can do business together.

On Mikhail Gorbachev, December 1984

◆

If you want to cut your own throat, don't come to me for a bandage.

To Robert Mugabe on South African sanctions, July 1986

◆

I cannot ever remember having spent so much time with another world leader. If he gave me his word, I would believe him.

On meeting Mikhail Gorbachev in Moscow, April 1987

◆

Ronnie, I was a fan of yours long before either of us entered politics. Kings Row, The Voice of the Turtle, The Hasty Heart they all made their way to Grantham.

Speech at dinner to President Reagan, 1991

◆

All right George, all right. But this is no time to go wobbly.

To George Bush, August 1990

◆

This man is a loser ... a person who has taken hostages cruelly, brutally, a person who has hidden behind the skirts of women and children.

On Saddam Hussein, 1990

◆

If we cannot visibly support him, then we shall be cheating future generations.

On Mikhail Gorbachev, 1990

◆

In the decade of the 80s, western values were placed in the crucible and they emerged with greater purity and strength. So much of the credit goes to President Reagan. Of him it can be said, as Canning said of Pitt, that he was the pilot that weathered the storm. The world owes him an enormous debt and it saddens me that there are some who refuse to acknowledge his achievements.

Speech to the American Conservative Institutes, 8 March 1991

◆

As leader of the Progressive Conservatives I thought he put too much emphasis on the adjective and not enough on the noun.

On former Canadian Prime Minister Brian Mulroney, 1993

◆

He would bully me, and I would bully him. Then it was: let's get down to business.

On Mikhail Gorbachev, BBC TV, 1993

◆

Your President, President Clinton, is a great communicator. The trouble is, he has absolutely nothing to communicate.

To American political observer Daniel Forrester, March 1994

◆

He does like women, you know.

On François Mitterrand

◆

We sometimes seem to be a partnership as indissolubly linked as Astaire and Rogers.

To Ronald Reagan at his 82nd-birthday party

◆

I was very disappointed that [Nelson Mandela] he confirmed armed struggle. Let me put it this way, the people who have achieved most in terms of political change in my generation have been the dissidents and refuseniks in the Soviet Union and in eastern Europe, they took a decision right at the beginning, they would never resort to violence, there are so many of them and thousands whose names we do not know, they would never resort to violence, never. And look what they have achieved. Similarly, look at Gandhi, you are quite right, those were the two things in the post-war generation, it was the non-violent that commands total respect from the whole world and has achieved far more than the violent movements. And I was deeply disappointed that he, and presumably others who adopt the ANC's beliefs, say armed violence. Armed violence means that you are prepared to kill and maim innocent men, women and children. In other words, you want more freedom and you are prepared to extinguish theirs and their lives in order to get your own. So I was very disappointed that they said the armed struggle. It means bombs and guns aimed at innocent people.

On Nelson Mandela, 21 February 1990

◆

We have lost a great President, a great American, and a great man, and I have lost a dear friend.

On the death of Ronald Reagan, 2004

◆

For the final years of his life, Ronnie's mind was clouded by illness. That cloud has now lifted. He is himself again, more himself than at any time on this Earth, for we may be sure that the Big Fellow upstairs never forgets those who remember him. And as the last journey of this faithful pilgrim took him beyond the sunset, and as heaven's morning broke, I like to think, in the words of Bunyan, that 'all the trumpets sounded on the other side'.

We here still move in twilight, but we have one beacon to guide us that Ronald Reagan never had. We have his example. Let us give thanks today for a life that achieved so much for all of God's children.

Eulogy for President Reagan, 11 June 2004

◆

We should remember Pope John Paul II not just as the greatest pope of modern times but also as a valiant fighter for the truth. His life was a long struggle against the lies employed to excuse evil. By combating the falsehoods of Communism and proclaiming the true dignity of the individual, his was the moral force behind victory in the Cold

War. Millions owe him their freedom and self-respect. The whole world is inspired by his example.

On the death of Pope John Paul II, 2005

◆

Saddam Hussein will never comply with the conditions we demand of him. His aim is, in fact, quite clear: to develop weapons of mass destruction so as to challenge us with impunity. How and when, not whether, to remove him are the only important questions.

On Saddam Hussein, 11 February 2002

◆

The wisest head and the broadest shoulders in Washington, a sure guide for past Presidents – and, I hope, a future one.

On George Shultz, 2000

WIT, WISDOM AND REGRETS

Oh you are saucy!

To photographers, who had asked her to move closer to Canadian
Prime Minister Pierre Trudeau

◆

Ronald Millar: (giving her encouragement before her
first speech to a Conservative Party Conference as party
leader) Piece of cake, Margaret.

Margaret Thatcher: Good heavens! Not now!

October 1975

◆

Sydney Bidwell MP: Is the Right Honourable Lady aware
that Mr Len Murray, the General Secretary of the TUC,
insists that when he sees her, it is like having a dialogue
with the deaf?

Margaret Thatcher: I had no idea that Mr Murray was
deaf.

◆

I confess that this is the biggest birthday party I have ever had. I just do not know whether my parents had in mind the timing of the party conference, but if that is what is meant by family planning I am all for it.

On her fifty-third birthday at the Conservative Party Conference,
13 October 1978

◆

James Callaghan: May I congratulate you on being the only man in your team.
Margaret Thatcher: That's one more than you've got in yours.

◆

Imagine a Labour canvasser talking on the doorstep to those East German families when they settle in on freedom's side of the wall. 'You want to keep more of the money you earn? I'm afraid that's very selfish. We shall want to tax that away. You want to own shares in your firm? We can't have that. The state has to own your firm. You want to choose where to send your children to school? That's very divisive. You'll send your child where we tell you.

13 October 1989

◆

What do you think of those two then?

> To male advisers, while holding up Page 3 of *The Sun* in front
> of them

◆

Jim Prior: I read in my paper you had developed a sexy voice.
Margaret Thatcher: Jim, what makes you think I wasn't
sexy before?

◆

Here's the man who turned down a date with me.

> To John Junor, after he had to turn down an invitation to Chequers

◆

Don't worry dear, don't worry. It could happen to anyone.

> To a Wren at Chequers who had just spilled gravy over Sir
> Geoffrey Howe

◆

Michael Portillo: I have to be hard on you, Mrs Thatcher,
because they will be. I have to be as tough as Fred Emery.
Margaret Thatcher: Oh, Michael, you're not like Fred
Emery. He's not clever.

> During the 1983 election campaign when the 25-year-old
> Michael Portillo was a campaign aide

◆

I really just begin to wonder what has happened to the
British sense of humour.

Responding to criticism of Kenny Everett's remarks about
bombing Russia, 8 June 1983

◆

Will this thing jerk me off?

While firing a field gun during a visit to the Falkland Islands,
January 1983

◆

Ronald Reagan: Margaret, if one of your predecessors had
been a little more clever...
Margaret Thatcher: I know, I know, I would have been
hosting this gathering.

At the 1983 Williamsburg Summit Dinner

◆

Denis Healey: You're going to cut and run.
Margaret Thatcher: The Right Honourable Gentleman is
afraid of an election is he? He is frightened, frightened, frit!

1983

◆

Interviewer: Why do people stop us in the street almost and tell us that Margaret Thatcher isn't just inflexible, she's not just single-minded, on occasions she's plain pig-headed and won't be told by anybody?

MT: Would you tell me who has stopped you in the street and said that?

Interviewer: Ordinary Britons...

MT: Where?

Interviewer: In conversation, in pubs...

MT (interrupting): I thought you'd just come from Belize.

Interviewer: Oh this is not the first time we've been here.

MT: Will you tell me who, and where and when?

Interviewer: Ordinary Britons in restaurants and cabs.

MT: How many?

Interviewer: ...in cabs

MT: How many?

Interviewer: I would say at least one in two

MT: Why won't you tell me their names and who they are?

Interview on Australian TV programme *60 Minutes*, 1981

◆

The trouble with you John, is that your spine does not reach your brain.

On Conservative backbencher John Whittingdale after being summoned to her room to urge MPs to vote against the Maastricht Treaty, 1992

◆

Being powerful is like being a lady. If you have to tell people you are, you aren't.

◆

Senator Daniel P. Moynihan: Prime Minister, you have not disappointed us. You are the first person we have seen today who has offered us a real drink.
Margaret Thatcher: [Picking up a whisky] One can only take so much orange juice!

After Indira Gandhi's funeral, October 1984

◆

Mr Dimbleby, there's no point in going on trying to prophesy what will happen. I don't believe in crystal balls and I do just remember that your own wasn't very good on election night.

27 November 1989

◆

I am always on the job.

Interview on *Aspel and Company*, LWT, 1984

◆

Has he resigned or has he gone for a pee?

To Cabinet colleagues on Michael Heseltine's resignation, January 1986

◆

Imagine what Labour would have done to them, those brave seafarers who risked all on the chance of success. Just imagine, had they been in power in those days. First, those merchant venturers who went out in the time of the first Elizabeth, they would have to be registered. Then they would have to enter into a planning agreement with the relevant Government department. After that there would be meetings with the Minister of Trade to decide which merchant would be allowed to venture and where. Then the National Investment Bank would have to decide who, if anyone, was allowed to invest in the fitting-out of the ship. And which pension fund was to be expected to risk its money. And then the TUC would have nominated fifty per cent of the representatives of any governing body to decide on a division of the profits, if there were any, after tax. The merchant venturer could then leave Britain, as long as he had cleared the voyage with the Foreign Investment Unit and satisfied the shop stewards that there were no non-union cabin boys on board. No wonder under Labour no one ventures. And friends if no one ventures, no one else gains.

Speech to Wembley Youth Rally, 5 June 1983

◆

I may be here, I may be twanging a harp.

Following a question from Sir Robin Day on whether she expected to still be Prime Minister in the year 2000, 12 June 1987

◆

A lot has happened since we last met. There was, for instance, our election victory in June. They tell me that makes it three wins in a row. Just like Lord Liverpool. And he was Prime Minister for fifteen years. It's rather encouraging.

Conservative Party Conference, 1987

◆

If it's one against forty-eight, I feel sorry for the forty-eight!

On the Commonwealth stance on South African sanctions

◆

I am not quite certain what my Right Honourable Friend said, but we both hold precisely the same view.

In the House of Commons, January 1989

◆

François Mitterrand: Shall we have a break now?
Margaret Thatcher: No, let's get on.

[The lights fuse and the room is plunged into darkness.]
Margaret Thatcher: Why can't we discuss the Social Chapter now?

At the EC Strasbourg summit, 1989

◆

Kenneth Clarke: Isn't it terrible about losing to the Germans at our national sport, Prime Minister?
Margaret Thatcher: I shouldn't worry too much – we've beaten them twice this century at theirs.

Following England's loss to Germany in the 1990 World Cup football semi-final

◆

Teacher to French primary school class: What is the name of the Queen of England?
Little girl: Elizabeth Thatcher?

Adapted from a letter to *The Independent*, 23 March 1990

◆

In the same period that the Americans have lived under one constitution our French friends notched up five. A Punch cartoon has a nineteenth-century Englishman asking a librarian for a copy of the French constitution, only to be told: 'I am sorry sir, we do not stock periodicals'.

Speech to the American Conservative Institutes, 8 March 1991

◆

Every Prime Minister needs a Willie.

On Willie Whitelaw, 1991

◆

It was so hard on the daffodils

After a woman had hit her on the head with some daffodils,
April 1992

◆

I'm in a dreadful hurry this morning. I've really only got time to explode.

A rare example of self-mockery to a group of her Ministers

◆

Why don't you sit down? You look far too drunk to stand up!

To a Lords Whip

◆

Margaret Thatcher: Did you ever practise at Chancery?
David Mellor: No.
MT: I thought so. Not clever enough.

◆

TV interviewer: Do you ever say to Mr Kinnock: You did very well today, Neil?
Margaret Thatcher: No, I've never had occasion to say that.

◆

Brian Walden: You come over as being someone who one of your backbenchers said is slightly off her trolley, authoritarian, domineering, refusing to listen to anybody else. Why? Why can you not publicly project what you have just told me is your private character?

Margaret Thatcher: Brian, if anyone's coming over as domineering in this interview, it's you. It's you.

◆

Margaret Thatcher: Are you telling me that the Royal Navy ships out there will be under the command of, did you say a Belgian or a Dutchman?

Admiral Fieldhouse: Well, yes Prime Minister, they're our NATO allies.

Margaret Thatcher: A foreigner? The Royal Navy under the command of a foreigner?

Admiral Fieldhouse: NATO allies, Prime Minister. We operate together all the time.

Margaret Thatcher: A foreigner? The Royal Navy? Quite impossible!

Preparing for the Gulf War, September 1990

◆

They [federalist European politicians] divide their time between court room, prison and debating chamber – giving a whole new meaning to the term 'conviction politician'.

Nicholas Ridley Memorial Lecture, 22 November 1996

◆

MT: John, Monty Python – are you sure he is one of us?
John Whittingdale: Absolutely, Prime Minister. He is a very good supporter.

Prior to the 1990 Conservative Party Conference speech

◆

We introduced the Community Charge. I still call it that. I like the Poles – I never had any intention of taxing them.

On the Poll Tax, Nicholas Ridley Memorial Lecture, 22 November 1996

◆

Protestors: Tories out, we want jobs!
MT: Never mind, it is wet outside. I expect that they wanted to come in. You cannot blame them; it is always better where the Tories are.

Conservative Party Conference, 1980

◆

I hope you won't mind, Mr President, my recalling that George Washington was a British subject until well after his fortieth birthday. I have been told, to my surprise, that he does not have a place in the British Dictionary of National Biography. I suppose the editors must have regarded him as a late developer.

Speech at a White House Dinner, 17 December 1979

◆

I heard voices getting all worked up about someone they kept calling the 'Prime Minister in Waiting' [Neil Kinnock]. It occurs to me, Mr President, that he might have quite a wait. I can see him now, like the people queuing up for the winter sales. All got up with his camp bed, hot thermos, woolly balaclava, CND badge... Waiting, waiting, waiting ... and then when the doors open, in he rushes – only to find that, as always, there's 'that woman' ahead of him again. I gather there may be an adjective between 'that' and 'woman' only no one will tell me what it is.

Conservative Party Conference, 1990

◆

I'll tell you something else: they [the Labour Party] don't stop at the front door.

Listen to this:

'Men and women should be able to share the rights and responsibilities of paid employment and domestic activities, so that job segregation within and outside the home is broken down.'

They're going to see that Denis does his share of the washing up.

Speech to Wembley Youth Rally, 1983

◆

You may have noticed there are many people who just can't bear good news. It's a sort of infection of the spirit and there's a lot of it about. In the eyes of these hand-wringing merchants of gloom and despondency, everything that Britain does is wrong. Any setback, however small, any little difficulty, however local, is seen as incontrovertible proof that the situation is hopeless.

Their favourite word is 'crisis'. It's crisis when the price of oil goes up and a crisis when the price of oil goes up and a crisis when the price of oil comes down. It's a crisis if you don't build new roads. It's a crisis when you do. It's a crisis if Nissan does not come here. And it's a crisis when it does.

It's being so cheerful as keeps 'em going.

Conservative Party Conference, 1986

◆

Now, that brings me to the Liberal Party. I gather that during the last few days there have been some ill-natured jokes about their new symbol, a bird of some kind, adopted by the Liberal Democrats at Blackpool. Politics is a serious business, and one should not lower the tone unduly. So I will say only this of the Liberal Democrat symbol and of the party it symbolises. This is an ex-parrot. It is not merely stunned. It has ceased to be, expired and gone to meet its maker. It is a parrot no more. It has rung down the curtain and joined the choir invisible. This is a late parrot.

Conservative Party Conference, 1990

◆

I notice that famous preacher, John Donne, always made just three points, and it's a very good rule. People can't usually digest more.

22 March 1992

THE DENOUEMENT: TREACHERY WITH A SMILE ON ITS FACE

Nigel is a very good Chancellor. Geoffrey is a very good Foreign Secretary – I'm not going any further.

May 1989

◆

I do not want you to raise the subject ever again. I must prevail.

To Nigel Lawson on joining the ERM, May 1989

◆

I'm making some changes, Geoffrey, and they will involve the Foreign Office.

To Sir Geoffrey Howe, 24 July 1989

◆

The Right Team for Britain's Future.

> Slogan for the 1989 Conservative Party Conference. Within thir-
> teen months five Cabinet Ministers had resigned

◆

Advisers advise, Ministers decide.

> On her relationship with Sir Alan Walters, 26 October 1989

◆

Nigel had determined that he was going to put in his
resignation. I did everything possible to stop him.

> October 1989

◆

Unassailable, unassailable.

> Description of Nigel Lawson in an interview with Brian Walden,
> 29 October 1989

◆

The day Nigel Lawson said 'enough' may be the day that
Mrs Thatcher's term of office started to draw to its close.

> *The Economist*, November 1989

◆

She could so easily have got rid of Walters, but increasingly I fear that she simply cannot bring herself to be on the losing side in any argument. That failing may ditch us all.

Willie Whitelaw, in a letter to Nigel Lawson following his resignation.

◆

By popular acclaim ... let me make it quite clear, I am very happy to carry on.

November 1989

◆

I have never been a lame duck in my life and I'm not going to start now. I shall go on as long as I have been elected.

27 November 1989

◆

Mrs Thatcher will find it much harder to win the next election than would another Conservative leader... Her policies are out of tune with the British people... Her European policy is disastrous.

Sir Anthony Meyer, 29 November 1989

◆

You are now in danger. This is not a little local difficulty, it's a crisis. Nigel has real standing in the party and you have rejected his advice, preferring to listen to Alan Walters... The party in the House won't like this at all.

Kenneth Baker to Margaret Thatcher following Nigel Lawson's resignation, 26 October 1989

◆

I am very pleased with the result. We can now get on with the real issue of tackling inflation. Prime Ministers have a lot of work to do. There is a great pile of it inside and it would be better now if I left you to get on with it.

Following her victory over Sir Anthony Meyer, 5 December 1989

◆

They wanted me to change my style of government, Nick. Why should I change my style of government? I am not going to.

To Nicholas Ridley, following a visit from the Executive of the 1922 Committee

◆

There are a hundred assassins lurking in the bushes, Prime Minister. Those people will come back and kill you.

Tristan Garel-Jones, following the victory over Sir Anthony Meyer, December 1989

◆

Carol Thatcher: Oh well, that's all over then.

Margaret Thatcher: Oh no, that's just the beginning.

Following the victory over Sir Anthony Meyer, December 1989

◆

History may tell how much Ian [Gow] did to lubricate the relationship between PM and Chancellor between 1979 and 1983. It was in the highest tradition of Wykehamist subtlety.

Peter Cropper, former Special Adviser to Sir Geoffrey Howe, 1990

◆

I'm still at the crease, though the bowling's been pretty hostile of late. And, in case anyone doubted it, can I assure you that there will be no ducking the bouncers, no stonewalling, no playing for time! The bowling's going to get hit all round the ground. That's my style.

Lord Mayor's Banquet, 12 November 1990

◆

I believe both the Chancellor and the Governor are cricketing enthusiasts so I hope there will be no monopoly of cricketing metaphors. It's rather like sending your opening batsmen to the crease only for them to find that before the first ball is bowled, their bats have been broken by the team captain... The time has come for others to consider their own response to the tragic conflict of loyalties with which I have myself wrestled for perhaps too long.

Sir Geoffrey Howe, resignation speech to the House of Commons,
13 November 1990

◆

Mrs Thatcher started with a look of tense composure and a faint smile. The composure held, the tension grew, and the smile disappeared.

Matthew Parris describing in *The Times* Mrs Thatcher's appearance during Sir Geoffrey Howe's resignation speech, 13 November 1990

◆

I was just amazed by the mixture of bile and treachery which just poured out. In a speech, every word of which had clearly been carefully drafted and in a speech, which he delivered, if I might say so, better than any speech I had ever heard him deliver. Perhaps this was his feelings coming to the fore... I had to sit with my back to him [Geoffrey Howe], I could have turned round to see him but I didn't particularly wish to. I knew the press were facing me in the gallery opposite me so I knew I must keep my features composed and calm. At the same time I was trying to assess the effect that speech would have because I knew some of the rumours and discussions which were taking place. It is an experience I would not wish to repeat.

In the end it was not my record which he assassinated. He assassinated his own character.

BBC TV, 1993

◆

Mrs Thatcher has been bitten by the man she treated as a doormat – and she deserves it.

Neil Kinnock, 13 November 1990

◆

She must go on.

John Major, 13 November 1990

◆

I am persuaded that I now have a better prospect than Mrs Thatcher of leading the Conservatives to a fourth electoral victory and preventing the calamity of a Labour Government.

Michael Heseltine, 14 November 1990

◆

In truth, it is difficult to run a campaign without the presence of the candidate.

Sir Norman Fowler

◆

After three general election victories, leading the only party with clear policies resolutely carried out, I intend to continue.

15 November 1990

◆

Journalist: Under no circumstances would you stand?
Douglas Hurd: Against her.

16 November 1990

◆

As proposer and seconder of the Prime Minister in the leadership election we both want to make it quite clear that what we wish to see is a good victory for Mrs Thatcher in the first and only ballot.

Statement by Douglas Hurd and John Major, 17 November 1990

◆

Mrs Thatcher deserves better than to be dismissed in the shoddy and demeaning manner some Tory MPs are minded to have in store for her.

Peregrine Worsthorne in the *Sunday Telegraph*, 18 November 1990

◆

If we win according to the rules, we win. The rules were not made by me. I abide by the rules. I expect others to abide by the rules.

Margaret Thatcher in an interview with the *Sunday Telegraph*, 18 November 1990

◆

We lost everything because we had gone too far to the left. We had strayed from every single thing we believed in. If you read Michael Heseltine's book, you will find it more akin to some of the Labour Party policies: intervention, corporatism, everything that pulled us down. There is a fundamental difference on economics and there's no point trying to hide it. Those of us who sat with Michael on economic discussions remember full well.

Margaret Thatcher in an interview with *The Times*, 19 November 1990

◆

Not, I'm afraid, as good as we had hoped.

Peter Morrison, about to give the results of the leadership election, 1990

◆

Prime Minister, it's here, this is the microphone.

BBC Political Correspondent, John Sergeant, outside the Paris
Embassy, November 1990

◆

I'm naturally very pleased that I got more than half the
parliamentary party and disappointed that it's not enough
to win on the first ballot so I confirm it is my intention to
let my name go forward for the second ballot.

Outside the Paris Embassy, November 1990

◆

The Prime Minister continues to have my full support
and I am sorry this destructive, unnecessary contest
should be prolonged in this way.

Douglas Hurd, outside the Paris Embassy, November 1990

◆

I fight on, I fight to win.

Upon leaving Downing Street for the Commons, 21 November
1990

◆

Now look here, you miserable little worm. You are in
this Cabinet because I put you there and for no other
reason. So I expect your support, and if I don't get it you

will be out of my Cabinet when I reshuffle it after all this nonsense is over.

Cecil Parkinson outlining what he thought Margaret Thatcher should have said to errant Ministers

◆

I was sick at heart. I could have resisted the opposition of opponents and potential rivals and even respected them for it; but what grieved me was the desertion of those I had always considered friends and allies and the weasel words whereby they had transmuted their betrayal into frank advice and concern for my fate.

The Downing Street Years, 1993

◆

What hurt most of all, was that this was treachery while I had been away at an international conference signing treaties on behalf of my country at the end of the Cold War. It was treachery with a smile on its face. Perhaps that was the worst thing of all.

Describing her betrayal by the Cabinet, BBC TV, 1993

◆

Margaret Thatcher: Will you please second my nomination?

[Long pause]

John Major: If that's what you want me to do, I'll do it.

◆

She may lose but she might win and if she's going to go down, she must go down fighting.

Alan Clark, 21 November 1990

◆

The fight is over. The battle is lost. You should withdraw from the field.

Kenneth Clarke, 21 November 1990

◆

Fuck the typing George, let's go and see her.

David Maclean to Sir George Gardiner, 21 November 1990

◆

We've come to bully you, Margaret.

Sir George Gardiner, in a vain attempt to persuade Mrs Thatcher to contest the second round of the leadership contest, 21 November 1990.

◆

Alan Clark: You're in a jam.

Margaret Thatcher: I know that.

AC: They're all telling you not to stand aren't they?

MT: I'm going to stand. I have issued a statement.

AC: That's wonderful. That's heroic. But the party will let you down.

MT: I am a fighter.

AC: Fight then. Fight right to the end, a third ballot if you need to, but you lose.

MT: It'd be so terrible if Michael won. He would undo everything I have fought for.

AC: But what a way to go! Unbeaten in three elections, never rejected by the people. Brought down by nonentities!

MT: But Michael ... as Prime Minister!

AC: Who the fuck's Michael? No one. Nothing. He won't last six months. I doubt if he'd even win the election. Your place in history is towering.

MT: Alan, it's been so good of you to come in and see me.

From Alan Clark's *Diaries*

♦

Darling, I don't want you to be humiliated.

Denis Thatcher, 21 November 1990

♦

It would have saved us an awful lot of bother if she had got four more votes.

Norman Tebbit

THE DENOUEMENT: RESIGNATION

Margaret Thatcher: Having consulted widely among colleagues ... [breaks down, wiping tears from her eyes] ... I am so sorry...

Cecil Parkinson: For God's sake, you read it, James.

Margaret Thatcher: [blows her nose] I have concluded that the unity of the party and the prospects of victory in the general election [breaks down again] ... will be better served if I stood down to enable Cabinet colleagues to enter the ballot for the leadership. I should like to thank all those in Cabinet and outside who have given me such dedicated support. It is vital that we stand together. The unity of the party is crucial and that's why I'm giving up. I couldn't bear all the things I have stood for over the past eleven years being rejected. The Cabinet must unite to stop Michael Heseltine.

Resignation statement to the Cabinet, 22 November 1990

◆

You have and will always continue to have the love and loyalty of the party. You have a special place in the heart of the party. You have led us to victory three times and you would have done so again. Those who have served you realise that they have been in touch with greatness.

Kenneth Baker at the Cabinet meeting, 22 November 1990

◆

This is a typically brave and selfless decision by the Prime Minister. Once again Margaret Thatcher has put her country and the party's interests before personal considerations. This will allow the party to elect a new leader to unite the party and build upon her immense success. If I could just add a personal note, I am very saddened that our greatest peacetime Prime Minister has left Government. She is an outstanding leader, not only of our country, but also of the world. I do not believe we will see her like again.

Kenneth Baker to reporters outside 10 Downing Street following the Cabinet meeting, 22 November 1990

◆

Rejoice, Rejoice!

Edward Heath, November 1990

◆

The Labour Party is led by a pygmy and we are led by a giant. We have decided that the answer to our problems is to find a pygmy of our own.

Cecil Parkinson, November 1990

◆

You don't take a decision like that without it being difficult. Without heartbreak. Heartbreak there may have been, but it was the right decision.

MT on her resignation during an interview with Michael Brunson, 1991

◆

Life begins at sixty-five.

Speech at the No. 10 farewell party, 26 November 1990

THE DENOUEMENT: I'M ENJOYING THIS!

On 22 November 1990, after already announcing she would stand down as Prime Minister, she faced a Motion of No Confidence in her Government tabled by the Leader of the Opposition, Neil Kinnock. It was arguably her best performance in the Commons chamber, and has gone down in history as one of the finest defences of a Government by a sitting Prime Minister. Thankfully the event was recorded and televised so it shall live on, below is an edited version of the Hansard transcript.

◆

The Prime Minister: It is, of course, the right and duty of Her Majesty's Opposition to challenge the position of the Government of the day. It is also their right to test the confidence of the House in the Government if they think that the circumstances warrant it. I make no complaint about that. But when the windy rhetoric of the Right Hon. Member for Islwyn (Mr Kinnock) has blown away, what are their real reasons for bringing this motion before the

House? There were no alternative policies – just a lot of disjointed, opaque words.

It cannot be a complaint about Britain's standing in the world. That is deservedly high, not least because of our contribution to ending the Cold War and to the spread of democracy through eastern Europe and the Soviet Union. It cannot be the nation's finances. We are repaying debts, including the debts run up by the Labour Party.

The Opposition's real reason is the leadership election for the Conservative Party, which is a democratic election according to rules which have been public knowledge for many years – one member, one vote. That is a far cry from the way in which the Labour Party does these things. Two in every five votes for its leader are cast by the trade union block votes, which have a bigger say than Labour Members in that decision: precious little democracy there.

The real issue to be decided by my Right Hon. and Hon. Friends is how best to build on the achievements of the 1980s, how to carry Conservative policies forward through the 1990s and how to add to three general election victories a fourth, which we shall surely win.

Eleven years ago, we rescued Britain from the parlous state to which Socialism had brought it. I remind the House that, under Socialism, this country had come to such a pass that [Nicholas Henderson] one of our most able and distinguished ambassadors felt compelled to write in a famous despatch, a copy of which found its way into *The Economist*, the following words: 'We talk of ourselves without shame as being one of the less prosperous countries of Europe. The prognosis for the foreseeable future', he said in 1979, was 'discouraging'.

Conservative Government has changed all that. Once again, Britain stands tall in the councils of Europe and of the world, and our policies have brought unparalleled prosperity to our citizens at home.

In the past decade, we have given power back to the people on an unprecedented scale. We have given back control to people over their own lives and over their livelihood – over the decisions that matter most to them and their families. We have done it by curbing the monopoly power of trade unions to control, even to victimise, the individual worker. Labour would return us to conflict, confrontation and government by the consent of the TUC. We have done it by enabling families to own their homes, not least through the sale of 1.25 million council houses. Labour opposes our new rents-to-mortgage initiative, which will spread the benefits of ownership wider still. We have done it by giving people choice in public services – which school is right for their children, which training course is best for the school leaver, which doctor they choose to look after their health and which hospital they want for their treatment.

Labour is against spreading those freedoms and choice to all our people. It is against us giving power back to the people by privatising nationalised industries. Eleven million people now own shares, and 7.5 million people have registered an interest in buying electricity shares. Labour wants to renationalise electricity, water and British Telecom. It wants to take power back to the state and back into its own grasp – a fitful and debilitating grasp.

Martin Flannery MP: The Right Hon. Lady says that she has given power back to the people, but more than 2 million of them are unemployed. Has she given power back to them? Inflation is 10.9 per cent. Is that giving power back to the people, compared with rates throughout the rest of Europe? Is the frittering away of £100 billion-worth of North Sea oil, which no other country has had, giving power back to the people? Will she kindly explain that – and how pushing many people into cardboard boxes and taking power away from them is somehow giving power back to them?

The Prime Minister: Two million more jobs since 1979 represent a great deal more opportunity for people. Yes, 10.9 per cent inflation is much higher than it should be, but it is a lot lower than 26.9 per cent under the last Labour Government. Yes, we have benefited from North Sea oil. The Government have made great investments abroad that will give this country an income long after North Sea oil has ceased. We have provided colossal investment for future generations. Labour Members ran up debts, which we have repaid. We are providing investment for the future; we do not believe in living at the expense of the future.

Dave Nellist MP: If things are as good as the Prime

Minister is outlining, why are her colleagues not happy for her to continue in the job of defending that record?

The Prime Minister: These are the reasons why we shall win a fourth general election. We have been down in the polls before when we have taken difficult decisions. The essence of a good Government is that they are prepared to take difficult decisions to achieve long-term prosperity. That is what we have achieved and why we shall handsomely win the next general election.

I was speaking of the Labour Party wanting to renationalise privatised industry. Four of the industries that we have privatised are in the top ten British businesses, but at the very bottom of the list of 1,000 British businesses lie four nationalised industries. Labour's industries consume the wealth that others create and give nothing back.

Because individuals and families have more power and more choice, they have more opportunities to succeed – 2 million more jobs than in 1979, better rewards for hard work, income tax down from 33p in the pound to 25p in the pound and no surcharge on savings income. Living standards are up by a third and 400,000 new businesses have been set up since 1979 – more than 700 every week. There is a better future for our children, thanks to our hard work, success and enterprise. Our people are better off than ever before.

The average pensioner now has twice as much to hand on to his children as he did eleven years ago. They are thinking about the future. This massive rise in our living standards reflects the extraordinary transformation of the private sector.

Simon Hughes MP: There is no doubt that the Prime Minister, in many ways, has achieved substantial success. There is one statistic, however, that I understand is not challenged, and that is that, during her eleven years as Prime Minister, the gap between the richest 10 per cent and the poorest 10 per cent in this country has widened substantially. At the end of her chapter of British politics, how can she say that she can justify the fact that many people in a constituency such as mine are relatively much poorer, much less well housed and much less well provided for than they were in 1979? Surely she accepts that that is not a record that she or any Prime Minister can be proud of.

The Prime Minister: People on all levels of income are better off than they were in 1979. The Hon. Gentleman is saying that he would rather that the poor were poorer, provided that the rich were less rich. That way one will never create the wealth for better social services, as we have. What a policy! Yes, he would rather have the poor poorer, provided that the rich were less rich. That is the Liberal policy. Yes, it came out. The Hon. Member did not intend it to, but it did.

The extraordinary transformation of the private sector has created the wealth for better social services and better pensions – it enables pensioners to have twice as much as they did ten years ago to leave to their children. We are no longer the sick man of Europe – our output and investment grew faster during the 1980s than that of any of our major competitors. Britain no longer has an overmanned, inefficient, backward manufacturing sector, but modern, dynamic industries.

The Right Hon. Gentleman referred to the level of inflation. Yes, in 1987 and 1988, the economy did expand too fast. There was too much borrowing, and inflation rose. That is why we had to take the tough, unpopular, measures to bring the growth of money supply within target. Inflation has now peaked and will soon be coming down. For the fundamentals are right. Our industry is now enterprising. It has been modernised and restructured. In sector after sector, it is our companies which lead the world – in pharmaceuticals, in telecommunications and in aerospace. Our companies have the freedom and talent to succeed – and the will to compete.

Jim Sillars MP: The Prime Minister is aware that I detest every single one of her domestic policies, and I have never hidden that fact. However, it is always a greater pleasure to tackle a political heavyweight opponent than a lightweight Leader of the Opposition.

Can I take the Prime Minister back to the question of the poor getting poorer? Does she not realise – even at this point, five minutes after midnight for her – that, because of the transfer of resources from the poor to the wealthy, the poll tax was unacceptable, and that it was because of the poll tax that she has fallen?

The Prime Minister: I think that the Hon. Gentleman knows that I have the same contempt for his Socialist policies as the people of east Europe, who have experienced them, have for theirs. I think that I must have hit the right nail on the head when I pointed out that the logic of those policies is that they would rather the poor were poorer. So long as the gap is smaller, they would rather have the poor poorer. One does not create wealth and opportunity that way. One does not create a property-owning democracy that way.

Yes, our companies have the freedom and talent to succeed, and the will to compete. And compete we must. Our competitors will not be taking a break. There must be no hankering after soft options and no going back to the disastrous economic policies of Labour Governments. No amount of distance lends enchantment to the lean years of Labour, which gave us the lowest growth rate in Europe, the highest strike record and, for the average family, virtually no increase in take-home pay. Labour's policies are a vote of no confidence in the ability of British people to manage their own affairs. We have that confidence. Confidence in freedom and confidence in enterprise. That is what divides Conservatives from Socialists.

Our stewardship of the public finances has been better than that of any Government for nearly fifty years. It has enabled us to repay debt and cut taxes. The resulting success of the private sector has generated the wealth and revenues which pay for better social services – to double the amount being spent to help the disabled, to give extra help to war widows, and vastly to increase spending on the National Health Service. More than 1 million more patients are being treated each year and there are 8,000 more doctors and 53,000 more nurses to treat them.

That is the record of eleven and a half years of Conservative Government and Conservative principles. All these are grounds for congratulation, not censure, least of all from the Leader of the Opposition, who has no alternative policies.

During the past eleven years, this Government have had a clear and unwavering vision of the future of Europe and Britain's role in it. It is a vision which stems from our deep-seated attachment to parliamentary democracy and commitment to economic liberty, enterprise, competition and a free market economy. No Government in Europe have fought more resolutely against subsidies, state aids to industry and protectionism; unnecessary regulation and bureaucracy and increasing unaccountable central power at the expense of national Parliaments. No Government have fought more against that in Europe than we have.

We have fought attempts to put new burdens and constraints on industry, such as the social charter which would take away jobs, in particular part-time jobs. For us, part of the purpose of the Community is to demolish trade barriers and eliminate unfair subsidies, so that we can all benefit from a great expansion of trade both within Europe and with the outside world.

The fact is that Britain has done more to shape the Community over the past eleven years than any other member state. We have worked for our vision of a Europe which is free and open to the rest of the world, and above all to the countries of eastern Europe as they emerge from the shadows of Socialism. It would not help them if Europe became a tight-knit little club, tied up in regulations and restrictions. They deserve a Europe where there is room for their rediscovered sense of nationhood and a place to decide their own destiny after decades of repression.

With all this, we have never hesitated to stand up for Britain's interests. The people of Britain want a fair deal in Europe, particularly over our budget contribution. We have got back nearly £10 billion which would otherwise have been paid over to the EC under the arrangements negotiated by the Labour Party when it was in power.

Indeed, what sort of vision does the Labour Party have? None, according to the Leader of the Opposition. Labour Members want a Europe of subsidies, a Europe of Socialist restrictions, a Europe of protectionism. They want it because that is how they would like to run – or is it ruin? – this country.

Every time that we have stood up and fought for Britain and British interests, Labour frontbench spokesmen have carped, criticised and moaned. On the central issues of Europe's future, they will not tell us where they stand. Do they want a single currency? The Right Hon. Gentleman does not even know what it means, so how can he know?

Neil Kinnock MP: It is a hypothetical question.

The Prime Minister: Absolute nonsense. It is appalling. He says that it is a hypothetical question. It will not be a hypothetical question. Someone must go to Europe and argue knowing what it means.

Are Labour members prepared to defend the rights of this United Kingdom Parliament? No, for all that the Right Hon. Gentleman said. For them, it is all compromise, 'sweep it under the carpet', 'leave it for another day', and 'it might sort itself out', in the hope that the people of Britain will not notice what is happening to them, and how the powers would gradually slip away.

We want the Community to move forward as twelve: and from my talks in Paris with other European leaders over the past few days, I am convinced that that is their aim too. Europe is strongest when it grows through willing cooperation and practical measures, not compulsion or bureaucratic dreams.

Alan Beith MP: Will the Prime Minister tell us whether she intends to continue her personal fight against a single currency and an independent central bank when she leaves office?

Dennis Skinner MP: No. She is going to be the governor.

The Prime Minister: What a good idea. I had not thought of that. But if I were, there would be no European central bank accountable to no one, least of all national parliaments. The point of that kind of Europe with a central bank is no democracy, taking powers away from every single Parliament, and having a single currency, a monetary policy and interest rates which take all political power away from us. As my Right Hon. Friend the Member for Blaby (Nigel Lawson) said in his first speech after the proposal for a single currency was made, a single currency is about the politics of Europe, it is about a federal Europe by the back door. So I shall consider the proposal of the Hon. Member for Bolsover (Dennis Skinner). Now where were we? I'm enjoying this, I'm enjoying this!

Michael Carttiss MP: Cancel it. You can wipe the floor with these people.

The Prime Minister: Yes, indeed – I was talking about Europe and the Socialist ideal of Europe. Not for us the corporatism, Socialism and central control. We leave those to the Opposition. Ours is a larger vision of a Community whose member states cooperate with one another more and more closely to the benefit of all.

Are we then to be censured for standing up for a free and open Britain in a free and open Europe? No. Our policies are in tune with the deepest instincts of the British people. We shall win the censure motion, so we shall not be censured for what is thoroughly right.

Under our leadership, Britain has been just as influential in shaping the wider Europe and the relations between East and West. Ten years ago, the eastern part of Europe lay under totalitarian rule, its people knowing neither rights nor liberties. Today, we have a Europe in which democracy, the rule of law and basic human rights are spreading ever more widely, where the threat to our security from the overwhelming conventional forces of the Warsaw Pact has been removed: where the Berlin wall has been torn down and the Cold War is at an end.

These immense changes did not come about by chance. They have been achieved by strength and resolution in defence, and by a refusal ever to be intimidated. No one in eastern Europe believes that their countries would be free had it not been for those western Governments who were prepared to defend liberty, and who kept alive their hope that one day east Europe too would enjoy freedom.

But it was no thanks to the Labour Party, or to the Campaign for Nuclear Disarmament of which the Right Hon. Gentleman is still a member. It is this Government who kept the nuclear weapons which ensured that we could never be blackmailed or threatened. When Brezhnev deployed the SS20s, Britain deployed the cruise missiles and was the first to do so. And all these things were done in the teeth of the opposition of the hon. Gentlemen opposite – and their ladies. The SS20s could never have been negotiated away without the bargaining strength which cruise and Pershing gave to the West. Should we be censured for our strength? Or should the Labour Party be censured for its weakness? I have no doubt that the people of Britain will willingly entrust Britain's security in future to a Conservative Government who defend them, rather than to Socialists who put expediency before principle.

Sir Eldon Griffiths MP: May I offer my Right Hon. Friend one measurement of the immense international respect and affection that she enjoys as a result of her policies of peace through strength? An opinion poll published on the west coast of America last month: the figures are

Gorbachev 74 per cent, Bush 75 per cent and Thatcher 94 per cent.

The Prime Minister: I am sure that they were quite right, too.

I wish to say a word or two about the situation in the Gulf, because it will dominate politics until the matter is resolved. It is principle which is at stake, as well as the rule of international law.

In my discussions with other heads of Government at the CSCE summit in Paris, I found a unanimous and impressive determination that Iraq's aggression must not succeed. The resolutions of the United Nations must be implemented in full. That is the peaceful option, Mr Speaker, and it is there to be taken, if Saddam Hussein so chooses. There was also a widespread recognition among my colleagues in Paris that the time was fast approaching when the world community would have to take more decisive action to uphold international law and compel Saddam Hussein to leave Kuwait.

No one can doubt the dangers which lie ahead. Saddam Hussein has many times shown his contempt for human life, not least for the lives of his own people. He has large armed forces. They are equipped with peculiarly evil weapons, both chemical and biological.

Twice in my time as Prime Minister we have had to send our forces across the world to defend a small country against ruthless aggression: first to our own people in the Falklands and now to the borders of Kuwait. To those who have never had to take such decisions, I say that they are taken with a heavy heart and in the knowledge of the manifold dangers, but with tremendous pride in the professionalism and courage of our armed forces.

There is something else which one feels. That is a sense of this country's destiny: the centuries of history and experience which ensure that, when principles have to be defended, when good has to be upheld and when evil has to be overcome, Britain will take up arms. It is because we on this side have never flinched from difficult decisions that this House and this country can have confidence in this Government today.

◆

Mr Kinnock, in all his years as Opposition leader, never let me down. On this occasion he delivered a speech that might have served if I had announced my intention to stand for the second ballot. It was a standard, partisan rant... He managed to fill me and the benches behind me with his own partisan indignation and therefore intensified the new-found Tory unity – in the circumstances a remarkable, if perverse achievement.

On Neil Kinnock's speech in the no confidence debate, *The Downing Street Years*, 1993

◆

It is impossible to follow the Prime Minister without soberly reflecting for a moment that we have heard what is probably the last of her important and considerable speeches from the Government despatch box. It was a bravura performance of the sort which she has made her own. I cannot with honesty say I shall miss it, but I shall certainly remember it and, as time intervenes, remember it with ever greater affection... It is impossible to have lived through last week without feeling that one is participating in a moment of history.

Paddy Ashdown, following Margaret Thatcher in the no confidence debate, 22 November 1990

◆

What she was doing was casting off all restraint and really shouting the things she had always wanted to shout but which people had advised her not to.

Edward Heath, *Independent on Sunday*, 23 January 1990

◆

We had a fantastic time. When it came to answering the Motion of No Confidence I felt it was no holds barred. I had beaten these people hollow for years and I thought now let me have one last go and we did. It was quite a go.

Interview with Barbara Walters, February 1991

◆

Ladies and Gentlemen,

We're leaving Downing Street for the last time after eleven and a half wonderful years, and we're very happy that we leave the United Kingdom in a very, very much better state than when we came here eleven and a half years ago.

It has been a tremendous privilege to serve this country as Prime Minister – wonderfully happy years – and I'm immensely grateful to the staff who supported me so well, and may I also say a word of thanks to all the people who sent so many letters, still arriving, and for all the flowers.

Now it's time for a new chapter to open and I wish John Major all the luck in the world. He'll be splendidly served and he has the makings of a great Prime Minister, which I'm sure he'll be in very short time.

Thank you very much. Goodbye.

Remarks departing Downing Street, 28 November 1990

TRIBUTES

When she came to power in 1979 we genuinely debated whether or not those who governed Britain would be the trade unions or the elected Government of our country. I think her most significant achievement is that that question is no longer asked. She has had a unique character and unique strengths and abilities and unique faults as well.

Paddy Ashdown, BBC TV News, 22 November 1990

◆

May I pay tribute to you on your decision this morning. You showed by that that you amount to more than those who have turned against you in recent days.

Neil Kinnock at Prime Minister's Questions, 22 November 1990

◆

She had a profound influence on President Reagan and particularly in his approach to what he had characterised as the evil empire. Five years later, if Margaret Thatcher, his close colleague and philosophical soulmate, is saying, 'Look, we can do business with this guy', that's very persuasive to President Reagan, I think. In fact, I know it was because I was there.

James Baker, BBC TV, 1993

◆

I think Mrs Thatcher did more damage to democracy, equality, internationalism, civil liberties, freedom in this country than any other Prime Minister this century. When the euphoria surrounding her departure subsides you will find that in a year or two's time there will not be a Tory who admits ever supporting her. People in the streets will say, thank God she's gone.

Tony Benn, *The Thatcher Factor*, Channel 4, December 1990

◆

It was a surprise. In our imagination she was the Iron Lady who would fight to the end. She was a historic figure who helped bring the Soviet Union closer to Europe.

Gennadi Gerasimov, Soviet Foreign Ministry spokesman, 22 November 1990

◆

I'll miss her because I value her counsel. I value her long experience and the wisdom that comes from that experience. She has been an outstanding Prime Minister for the United Kingdom and an outstanding friend to the United States.

President George Bush, 22 November 1990

♦

Margaret Thatcher was the hardest-working head of Government I ever met. Her application was prodigious and she was always extraordinarily well briefed for every meeting. Whatever the subject, she could press her sometimes jarring and belligerent viewpoints with great authority, and for that I deeply respected her.

Bob Hawke, Australian Prime Minister 1983–91

♦

She has made a remarkable contribution to Britain's history and has led this country with great distinction in the 1980s.

Michael Heseltine, BBC TV News, 22 November 1990

♦

The Iron Lady was a great lady. She deserves applause.

Valéry Giscard d'Estaing, 22 November 1990

◆

I think we were all shocked, and the President [Jacques Delors] immediately said his overwhelming feeling was of one of the highest esteem of the Prime Minister despite the differences and disagreements.

Sir Leon Brittan, 22 November 1990

◆

Margaret Thatcher was beyond argument a great Prime Minister. Her tragedy is that she may be remembered less for the brilliance of her many achievements than for the recklessness with which she later sought to impose her own increasingly uncompromising views.

Sir Geoffrey Howe, 1994

◆

It is quite clear that history will record that Margaret Thatcher was the greatest Prime Minister this country has had since Churchill.

Nigel Lawson, *The Times*, 23 November 1990

◆

I should like to thank you for the great cooperation and friendship which you have shown me during our time together in office during which so much has been achieved.

Charles Haughey, Irish Prime Minister, in a letter, November 1990

◆

You are always welcome in Czechoslovakia.

Václav Havel

◆

So long Maggie, we want you to know
We still love you, even though you must go;
We'll all miss you, when you leave No. 10,
So farewell Maggie, but come back again.
They say a week in politics
Can be a long wait,
But you stayed on eleven years
And made Great Britain great.

Max Bygraves, LBC *Newstalk*, 26 November 1990

◆

You have done more than any of us ever thought possible
and ever hoped to do. You were a great leader, a giant – a
beautiful giant.

Sir Keith Joseph, 26 November 1990

◆

She has been a strong and courageous Prime Minister, always sustained by her Christian faith. I pray that her experience and gifts may continue to be at the service of the nation.

Archbishop of Canterbury Dr Robert Runcie, *The Times,* 23 November 1990

◆

Mrs Thatcher will be remembered not as a great executive leader, because every Prime Minister is powerful, but because she is a teacher. The weakness of the Labour Party over a long period is that it hasn't done any teaching.

Tony Benn, 8 February 1992

◆

I should like to offer my heartfelt tribute, on behalf of so very many, to our fine leader of yore, on the day, remembered throughout the world, when a much revered lady stood down, apparently at the request of her party, with dignity and grace.

Judith Gardner from Oxford, in a letter to the *Sunday Telegraph,* 22 November 1992

◆

You are the only person so far to whom has been awarded the Order of the Handbag.

George Shultz to Margaret Thatcher at his farewell party, December 1992

◆

She's the Prime Minister who really wanted to be Queen. Major's boring, the Prime Minister who wanted to be a train spotter.

Thatcher impersonator Steve Nallon, BBC TV, 1993

◆

My admiration for Mrs Thatcher is extremely high. She is imposing and articulate, an ideological politician instead of a compromiser. She was a great Prime Minister and her influence was felt around the world.

Vice President Dan Quayle, 1994

◆

The nation was oppressed by many dragons in 1979. Margaret Thatcher came forth to slay them. After she had slain them the nation no longer had need of her. Normal, humdrum government has been resumed. We shall miss her style of government.

Nicholas Ridley, 1991

◆

Her influence was very constructive, so I was always glad to see her coming. As a matter of fact, sometimes when I was trying to persuade the President of something that I knew she agreed with but he was reluctant about I was shameless in saying, 'Mr President, here's what Margaret Thatcher says on that subject. She's looked into it, so hear me out on this.'

George Shultz, BBC TV, 1993

◆

I think her greatest achievement is to have made people believe that the impossible is possible. That the things which were said in 1979 to be beyond resolution, the problem of the trade unions for example, she boldly took it on and she did it. If politicians can learn that lesson from her, that there is no problem which is too big to be solved, then she's contributed something enormously important to our life.

Norman Tebbit, *The Thatcher Factor*, Channel 4, December 1990

◆

A rare leader who had strong beliefs and revitalised the United Kingdom.

Toshiki Kaifu, Japanese Prime Minister, 22 November 1990

◆

I think the rest of the world will think we're mad, and indeed we are. We've turned out the greatest Prime Minister in the post-war years simply because of short-term nerves.

Ann Widdecombe, BBC TV News, 22 November 1990

◆

We have lost a leader who shared our views and for whom we had tremendous admiration, love and respect.

Nicholas Bennett, a member of the Thatcherite No Turning Back group of MPs, 22 November 1990

◆

We would find it rather difficult to do that.

German Government spokesman when asked for a tribute to Margaret Thatcher, 22 November 1990

◆

I am horrified, I am disgusted with the Tory Party. I think it is tantamount to committing political suicide that we have put on one side and forced to resign the greatest political leader in the United Kingdom this century.

Nicholas Winterton MP, BBC TV News, 22 November 1990

◆

A remarkable lady, an extraordinary personality who I am sure will go down in history as one of the more significant British Prime Ministers.

Henry Kissinger, 22 November 1990

◆

The gentlemen in grey suits should now be visited by gentlemen in white coats.

Letter to *The Times*, 23 November 1990

◆

We do not have to like our political leaders; we must respect them. Margaret Thatcher can never be accused of courting popularity; nobody, however, commands more respect in rank and file Tories at home or among other world leaders. It is a tragedy for Britain that she has decided to resign.

Letter to *The Times*, 26 November 1990

◆

A lady sent to us on wings from heaven.

Rocco Forte

◆

She was a tigress surrounded by hamsters.

John Biffen, *The Observer*, December 1990

◆

The further you got from Britain, the more admired you found she was.

James Callaghan, *The Spectator*, December 1990

◆

The greatest Briton since Winston Churchill.

Charles Price, 1991

LIFE AFTER DOWNING STREET

Now it is time for a new chapter to begin and I wish John Major all the luck in the world.

On the steps of 10 Downing Street as she left it for the last time, 27 November 1990

◆

It's a funny old world.

At a Cabinet meeting following her resignation, 27 November 1990

◆

The same person in a slightly different capacity will be available to serve Great Britain in whatever way it happens.

22 November 1990

◆

That thing in November.

The phrase Lady Thatcher is reputed to use when referring to the leadership election and her resignation

◆

It is the move I would have least wanted to do.

Michael Gerson, head of the removal company that moved the Thatchers from Downing Street to Dulwich

◆

I shan't be pulling the levers, but I shall be a very good back-seat driver.

On her role following her departure from No. 10, 1990

◆

I have done pretty well out of being Mrs Thatcher.

On what she should be called following the award of a baronetcy to Denis Thatcher

◆

She will need people close to her, to help her and to wipe the tears, because there will be some, whether real or metaphorical.

Professor Cary Cooper

◆

You told me that I would have had to do something about the Community Charge. I would have found that difficult. You also told me that I would have had to ring up MPs and spend my time in the tea room. That's not for me after eleven years.

To Kenneth Baker a week after her resignation

◆

I wouldn't change any of my policies if I had my time again, and no, no, no, I don't spend my time regretting.

Independent on Sunday, 16 January 1990

◆

Sometimes I say, 'Which day is it?' I never said that at No. 10.

11 May 1991

◆

Home is where you come to when you've nothing better to do.

11 May 1991

◆

I can defend it clearly, explicitly at any time, in any place and to any person.

On the Community Charge (Poll Tax), 8 June 1991

◆

I've been very quiet at home, which has been a very great effort on my part. A little less silence might be called for on my part.

Speaking about Europe, 22 June 1991

◆

I shall go on doing things until I march up to the Pearly Gates and say, I've come – have you got any work for me yet?

The Independent, 6 July 1991

◆

The worst thing is the realisation that some of those who you most trusted were most prominent in your betrayal.

Speaking after the coup against Mikhail Gorbachev, 31 August 1991

◆

I found that she was not at all bitter. She was really rather stunned. She couldn't quite believe it had happened and she couldn't quite understand how it had happened. But she is a very practical person and she had to get on with the business of organizing her life.

Cecil Parkinson, *World in Action*, 11 November 1991

◆

At times she suddenly seemed to lose focus. It was like seeing a dear friend under sedation.

Lord Gowrie, 1991

◆

It's a traumatic shock, it really is. You don't realise until you're out. Even now when we're driving down Whitehall my mind still thinks we'll turn right into Downing Street, then I realise we're not going to. And then you realise it's not you any more.

Interview with Barbara Walters, February 1991

◆

I see a tendency to try to undermine what I achieved and to go back to more powers for Government. That would be totally wrong for a proud and free people.

Interview with Barbara Walters, February 1991

◆

I think it is wrong to have a contest for the leadership while you're Prime Minister. I am the first Conservative Prime Minister who has been subject to that. I don't think it does any good for the office of Prime Minister. I hope they'll never have it again. I think it is wrong.

Interview with Barbara Walters, February 1991

◆

I have never been defeated by the people. It is my great pride.

Interview with Barbara Walters, February 1991

♦

It is my purpose to continue to be a strong ally and friend of Prime Minister Major and the Government he leads.

After announcing she would stand down at the 1992 general election, June 1991

♦

The enjoyment of the backbenches comes from being able to speak out freely. This, however, I knew would never again be possible. My every word would be judged in terms of support for or opposition to John Major. I would inhibit him just by my presence, and that in turn would inhibit me.

On her decision not to stand in the 1992 general election, *The Path to Power*, 1995

♦

Major is doing wonders.

Interview with Barbara Walters, February 1992

♦

It's quite a wrench. I shan't realise it fully until after the election night and after the assembly of Parliament.

On standing down as MP for Finchley, 28 March 1992

◆

I think Essex Man will vote for a Conservative Government.

During the general election campaign, 4 April 1992

◆

I do not accept the idea that all of a sudden Major is now his own man. There isn't any such thing as Majorism.

25 April 1992

◆

It's very nervy. It's such a hot day, too hot to be wearing such heavy clothes.

Upon taking her seat in the House of Lords, 30 June 1992

◆

It is a privilege to take my place on these distinguished, tranquil benches after thirty-three years before the mast in another place.

Her first words to the House of Lords, 2 July 1992

◆

I calculate that I was responsible for proposing the elevation to the Lords of some 214 of its present numbers.

House of Lords, 2 July 1992

◆

I have never knowingly made a non-controversial speech in my life.

2 July 1992

◆

I never felt the need for a virility symbol.

On the eve of the French referendum on the Maastricht Treaty,
26 September 1992

◆

I was sick at heart. I could have resisted the opposition of opponents and potential rivals and even respected them for it; but what grieved me was the desertion of those I had always considered friends and allies and the weasel words whereby they had transmuted their betrayal into frank advice and concern for my fate.

The Downing Street Years, 1993

◆

I have been in Parliament for thirty-four years. I cannot remember a time when politicians were so out of touch with the people and so in touch with each other.

18 April 1993

◆

You can't lead an 'if only' life. There's always a future, there's always work. I shall work till my dying day.

23 October 1993

◆

Life is a choice of alternatives and in my view John is the best of the three.

BBC Radio 2, 24 October 1993

◆

I understand now that those marvellous working miners, the Democratic Union, feel a sense of betrayal.

On the Government's pit closure plans, 30 October 1993

◆

I've just had the honour of delivering the speech at Ronald Reagan's 84th-birthday celebrations. I'm only sixty-nine. Just the age Ronald was when he became President, and I must say I'm feeling a little underemployed.

7 February 1995

◆

They have hit at everything I believed in.

On the Major Government, 12 June 1995

◆

Insofar as we are down in the opinion polls it is because we have not been Conservative enough.

17 June 1995

◆

I don't think I was unkind to him. I supported him a lot – I chose him!

Referring to John Major, 23 June 1995

◆

I cannot leave the future alone. I don't want it to go wonky or wobbly.

24 June 1995

◆

In Britain, we're all Thatcherites now.

At a party in the United States given in honour of her seventieth birthday, 24 October 1995

◆

Get cracking.

Urging Conservatives to support John Major, 9 October 1996

◆

I am so pleased that after four election defeats they have now come to terms with the 1980s. Perhaps after four more they will come to terms with the 1990s. I am told we are all Thatcherites now. My goodness me, never has the road to Damascus been so congested.

Daily Telegraph, 9 December 1996

◆

You became President at the age of sixty-nine and to serve for two terms is – well, quite an incentive to those of us about to start a new career late in life.

At President Reagan's eightieth birthday, 1991

◆

I cut back the powers of Government. Now they've got to be jolly careful they don't give Government too many extra powers and undo what I've done.

On the Major Government, 27 April 1992

◆

There isn't such a thing as Majorism.

27 April 1992

◆

When I came to this House it was somehow under the impression that things were less lively here, much more courteous and much less robust. I find that it is not so and I am delighted.

On the House of Lords, 7 June 1993

◆

The collapse of the Evil Empire is the greatest and best political development of my adult lifetime.

Speech to the National Press Club, 5 November 1993

◆

We might have avoided the worst atrocities of Nazism had we learnt the lessons of the First World War that the price of freedom is eternal vigilance.

18 May 1994

◆

Just as in medicine, viruses develop new virulent strains which have to be overcome, so in politics new tyrants await to test our resolve, and new problems arise to challenge our will.

Speech to Buckingham University, 18 May 1994

◆

It is lovely to be back at this address – which I still think of as home... Though, come to think of it, Gladstone did form his fourth administration when he was over eighty. So you have much to look forward to.

At a No. 10 dinner marking her seventieth birthday

◆

I haven't changed. Well, you wouldn't expect me to, would you?

26 September 1995

◆

They tell me I have become an 'ism' in my own lifetime. I didn't know quite how to take that to start with. But they assure me it's a compliment – one of the better 'isms'. They say all sorts of things about you when you've left office. They don't always wait for that. Do they, John?

26 September 1995

◆

So to those who say it's time to ease up, to relax and to give the other side a chance, I say (if I may coin a phrase): 'NO!' 'NO!' 'NO!'

26 September 1995

◆

A hung Parliament would hang the future of our country. Just look at some countries that have had coalition Governments. You may have read about Belgium in the papers in the last few weeks. It took them 100 days to form a new Government. What would have happened if anything vital had come up during that time? Did it help their main decisions? Did it help their deficit to come down? Not a bit of it. They've got one of the worst deficits in Europe. Not surprising with a coalition Government. No one has got the guts to stand up and say no to public expenditure. So they get a big deficit. Does continuous coalition government help them to stand up against the tyrant? No. When we wanted to buy munitions they wouldn't sell them to us. So, do not go for coalitions – ever.

22 March 1992

◆

The whole of Mr Blair's strategy in creating the boneless wonder that calls itself New Labour is to reassure the electorate in its illusion.

On New Labour, 1 April 1997

◆

US journalist: Back in the States people are thinking about Tony Blair as the new Margaret Thatcher. What do you think about that?
MT: Well I think they have got the sex wrong for a start. And I think they have got the willpower wrong. I think

they have got the reasoning wrong. I think they have got the strength wrong.

9 April 1997

♦

The fightback begins now!

In a telephone conversation with Michael Portillo the day after the 1997 general election

♦

The true way to give the Scots more control over their future is, by contrast, to cut back what Government spends and controls, leaving more freedom of choice for the people. That, though, is the last thing which so many still Socialist-minded Scottish politicians want.

9 September 1997

♦

I do not believe that most Scots want to end the Union. But separation is the destination towards which the present devolution proposals lead. They represent a negation of our shared history and an abdication of our joint future. Scottish voters can do no greater service to their country than to reject them.

On the devolution referendum, *The Scotsman*, 9 September 1997

♦

In Britain, we have been enduring one of the worst summers on record. And I'm talking about the Government, as well as the weather.

19 July 2000

◆

Obviously this is a very disappointing result. But let me say this. William Hague campaigned tirelessly from first to last. He was a bonny fighter. But make no mistake, the Conservative Party will be back.

On the resignation of William Hague, 8 June 2001

◆

I was told beforehand my arrival was unscheduled, but on the way here I passed a local cinema and it turns out you were expecting me after all. The billboard read *The Mummy Returns*.

Conservative Party Conference, 22 May 2001

◆

Today's Labour Party has no discernible principles at all. It is rootless, empty and artificial. And when anything real or human surfaces despite the spin – it's the bitter, brawling, bully that we hoped we'd seen the last of twenty years ago.

22 May 2001

◆

Ken Clarke has many qualities. But I have no doubt that Iain Duncan Smith would make infinitely the better leader. I am confident that, if elected leader, Iain will restore the Conservative Party's faith and fortunes. He deserves support.

Endorsing Iain Duncan Smith for leader of the Conservative Party, 2001

◆

Over recent months Lady Thatcher has suffered a number of small strokes. After thorough investigation involving a number of tests, her doctors have told her that these can neither be predicted nor prevented. They have therefore told her to cut back her programme at once and in particular to avoid the undue strain that public speaking places on her. With great regret, she has decided to abide by this advice and to cancel all her speaking engagements.

Statement announcing her withdrawal from public speaking, 22 March 2002

◆

The new dogma about climate change has swept through the left-of-centre governing classes ... and provides a marvellous excuse for worldwide, supra-national Socialism.

Statecraft, 2003

◆

I might have preferred iron, but bronze will do. It won't rust. And, this time I hope, the head will stay on.

Unveiling her statue in Parliament, after a previous marble one was decapitated, 22 February 2007

◆

'Ah, Liberals. We should abolish of few of them. No one shall abolish me.'

On the Coalition Government's attempt to reform the House of Lords, July 2012

ACCORDING TO CONSERVATIVES

The only occasion on which I thought it necessary to seek to guide her in the House was when she had scored in quick succession off [David] Marquand and [Richard] Crossman, and was joyfully following this up. I then said, 'Margaret, I know you are enjoying yourself, but do remember that the object is to get the Bill through!'

John Boyd-Carpenter, Margaret Thatcher's Secretary of State at the Ministry of Pensions and National Insurance 1961–62

♦

This one is different. Quite exceptionally able, a first-class brain.

Iain Macleod

♦

Mark my words, Margaret Thatcher will be the next leader of the party.

Lord Margadale, 1972. His son, Peter Morrison, later became her Parliamentary Private Secretary

◆

I have kissed her often before [but not] on a pavement outside a hotel in Eastbourne.

Willie Whitelaw, after a kiss for the benefit of reporters during the Conservative Party leadership election campaign, February 1975

◆

It wasn't an election. It was an assumption.

Norman St John-Stevas on Mrs Thatcher's election as leader of the party, 1975

◆

In excluding me from the shadow Cabinet, Margaret Thatcher has chosen what I believe to be the only wholly honest solution and one which I accept and welcome.

Edward Heath, February 1975

◆

I wouldn't say she was open-minded on the Middle East so much as empty headed. For instance, she probably thinks that Sinai is the plural of sinuses.

Jonathan Aitken

◆

We must create the new history for tomorrow's traditions.

Norman Strauss to Margaret Thatcher, 1977

◆

I wouldn't treat my gamekeeper the way that woman treated me.

Christopher Soames following his sacking from the Cabinet, 1981

◆

The trouble is, we've got a corporal at the top, not a cavalry officer.

Francis Pym

◆

Prime Minister, you are talking too much.

A note from Lord Carrington to Margaret Thatcher during a meeting with the Chinese Prime Minister

◆

She has provided the best leadership of any Prime Minister since Winston Churchill and she deserves the support of every patriotic citizen.

Reg Prentice, 1981

♦

Margaret Thatcher and Ted Heath both have a great vision. The difference is that Margaret Thatcher has a vision that Britain will one day be great again, and Ted Heath has a vision that one day Ted Heath will be great again.

Robert Jones MP, 1981

♦

She cannot see an institution without hitting it with her handbag.

Julian Critchley, 1982

♦

I was struck by her incisiveness in everything she said and her grasp of her subject. She was never caught out, ever, by any question asked. So my recollection of her is quite clear. Curiously enough I came back one day and said to my wife, 'You know, she's got the brains of all of us put together, so we'd better look out'.

Lord Home on Mrs Thatcher in the Heath Government, 1985

◆

Shut up, Prime Minister.

> Nigel Lawson, after Mrs Thatcher continually interrupted Sir
> Keith Joseph at a Cabinet meeting.

◆

I think it was much more a peasants' uprising than a
religious war. It was seen much more as the overthrow of
the tyrant king rather than a great ideological shift.

> Chris Patten on Mrs Thatcher's election as leader of the
> party, 1985

◆

I tell you something she's not very good at; she's not very
good at relaxing, taking time off. That's the nature of the
creature. God Bless her, I think.

> Sir Keith Joseph, 1985

◆

I think Churchill would be appalled at the Thatcher
Government.

> Edward Heath

◆

She's the only party leader I can think of, certainly in the post-war period, who's been more radical in Government than in opposition.

Chris Patten, 1985

◆

Whatever the lady does is wrong. I do not know of a single right decision taken by her.

Edward Heath

◆

To be loyal means 100 per cent acceptance of Government thinking: any dissent, or even admittance of doubt, is treachery and treason. After nine years as party leader and five as Prime Minister, Margaret Thatcher still asks the question, 'Are you one of us?', by which she means, 'Are you completely free of any doubt as to the utter rightness of everything we are doing?' It will come as no surprise that I am not 'one of us'.

Francis Pym, 1986

◆

Working with a team is not her strong point.

David Howell

◆

She was like Boudicca, hammering away at those wicked people seeking to carry out policies alien to her trusted beliefs and nature.

James Prior

◆

You've got to put her in the same category as Bloody Mary, Queen Elizabeth I, Queen Anne and Queen Victoria. However, she reminds me most of Queen Elizabeth I out of these four. Her handling of men is not dissimilar. I mean, if you had been a courtier of Queen Elizabeth I you would never have known quite whether you were going to get the treatment of an admired friend, or a poke in the eye with an umbrella.

Lord Hailsham

◆

Although the advice that you get if you get to see Margaret is 'stand up for yourself, shout back, and argue the toss and then she will respect you', the trouble is that sort of advice to the English middle-class male of a certain age doesn't actually help us very much because we've always been brought up to believe that it's extremely rude to shout back at women.

Julian Critchley, 1985

◆

Everyone likes to win arguments. She likes to win them more than most.

Willie Whitelaw, 1985

◆

The truth of the matter is that in my experience she was almost always right and therefore there wasn't a great necessity for her to admit she was wrong.

Ian Gow

◆

She is a very patient person. She can put up for a long time with being made to say what she doesn't believe.

Enoch Powell

◆

I never thought of her as a woman.

John Biffen

◆

She made up her mind really quite a long time ago that the country's future was damaged, really, by the trade unions, and she made up her mind to deal with that. And she made up her mind that inflation was the worst enemy of progress. And the two things, of course, were connected because trade union activities led to an increase in costs.

And she did them both... I think she felt her instincts were right and made up her mind to follow them, and in the course of that has done on the whole very well.

Lord Home, November 1988

◆

History will surely recognise her achievements as Britain's first woman Prime Minister, a leader with the courage of her convictions, who assailed the conventional wisdom of her day, challenged and overthrew the existing order, changed the political map, and put her country on its feet again.

Sir Geoffrey Howe, May 1989

◆

Tim Bell: It's up to you, you must tell her very firmly that she should stand down.
Gordon Reece: I can't. I love her.
Denis Thatcher: Steady on, she's my wife!

1989

◆

She'll be Prime Minister until the middle of the next century.

Jeffrey Archer, 1989

◆

Some people find it difficult to argue with a woman Prime Minister and shrivel up.

Douglas Hurd, BBC TV, 30 October 1989

◆

I wish that old cow would resign.

Richard Needham, caught out on a mobile phone, 1990 – he later said sorry

◆

May I say that my Right Honourable Friend the Prime Minister is looking jolly nice today?

Edwina Currie at Prime Minister's Questions just after announcing she thought the Prime Minister should retire, July 1990

◆

She was at all times a politician and I was never entirely sure how much the saloon bar xenophobia of her later years represented her own uninhibited feelings and how far she saw it as a potential vote winner.

Nigel Lawson

◆

On the issue of Europe Mrs Thatcher has very strong views
and I understand those views. I do not share many of them.

Michael Heseltine, 17 November 1990

◆

I am always there if she needs me and if I need her advice
I would certainly approach her.

Gerald Bowden, Mrs Thatcher's local MP in Dulwich, December
1990

◆

I was frequently embarrassed by the way Margaret
conducted herself within the European Community. Her
tactics were counter-productive and damaging to the
UK's interests. On most issues her approach was foolish.
Her style and tone of voice came to irk the others so much
that they instinctively sank their differences and joined
forces against her.

Nigel Lawson

◆

She carried the cult of the individual much too far and has
done us terrible damage in Europe with her fishwife yell-
ing and screaming.

Nicholas Soames

◆

Thatcherism is what you make of it. It was a knowledge that Butskellism did not work, but that one could not adopt market economics and patriotism without having a clear idea of what they entail. Thatcherism's mood was one of impatience with what was going on, the feeling that there were too many Old Etonians around. In the beginning was the mood, and the mood became Thatcher. It was essentially beliefs, not ideas.

Sir Alfred Sherman, April 1990

◆

Not one of our economic achievements would have been possible without the courage and the leadership of the Prime Minister. And, if I may say so, they possibly derived some little benefit from the presence of a Chancellor who wasn't exactly a wet himself.

Sir Geoffrey Howe, *The Independent*, 14 November 1990

◆

I am not running as Son of Margaret Thatcher. I have my own priorities and my own programmes.

John Major, *The Times*, 25 November 1990

◆

You don't have to leave No. 10 in tears.

Edward Heath, *Independent on Sunday*, 23 January 1990

◆

I've always had a great respect and been very candid with her, and I hope the reverse is the case.

Chris Patten, 1990

◆

Margaret Thatcher drove us like there was no tomorrow. But I think there is a genuine feeling now that this macho, workaholic, earn lots of money way of life has run its course. There has been a shift in attitude. People are looking for a more balanced approach.

Edwina Currie on MPs' working hours, *Independent on Sunday*, 29 January 1991

◆

She is a formidable politician. She has always spoken her mind. She has a right to do it and she will continue to do so.

John Major, 29 June 1991

◆

Anyone who supposed that when Margaret Thatcher left No. 10 she was going to take a Trappist vow did not know that formidable politician.

Chris Patten, December 1991

◆

As Margaret Thatcher came up in the world, so the Conservative Party came down.

Julian Critchley, BBC TV, 1991

◆

What has made her a Prime Minister whom so many of us admire is that she has a deep ideological sincerity. She believes. She is not there for herself at all. She is there because she believes we've got it all wrong in terms of ideology in this country. And she's right.

Lord Vinson

◆

Mrs Thatcher was not lightly bullied.

Michael Heseltine, November 1991

◆

Do you know what Margaret Thatcher did in her first budget? Introduced VAT on yachts! It somewhat ruined my retirement.

Edward Heath, 28 November 1992

◆

Mrs Thatcher categorised her Ministers into those she
could put down, those she could break down and those
she could wear down.

Kenneth Baker, *The Independent*, 11 September 1993

◆

Was I ever one of us?

Kenneth Baker to Charles Powell, BBC TV, September 1993

◆

She came to respect me, you know. She trusted me the
longer I was there. I did some difficult things for her. I
could deliver. I came to like her. I suppose I began to like
her when she made me a Cabinet Minister. It was a very
great honour.

Kenneth Baker, BBC TV, September 1993

◆

We were all her creation.

Kenneth Baker, BBC TV, September 1993

◆

It was like losing my mother. My mother is still alive but
one day she won't be, and when that occurs it will, I suspect,
be exactly like the day that Margaret Thatcher resigned.

Michael Brown, *Daily Telegraph*, 25 October 1993

◆

There were moments when Mrs Thatcher would privately rage so ferociously against something the Government had done that you almost forgot she was Prime Minister.

David Mellor, *The Independent*, 4 March 1995

◆

I admired Margaret Thatcher hugely, but whenever you went near her, the stink of sycophancy was overwhelming. And she liked toffs, which I patently was not.

Steven Norris, 25 March 1995

◆

She has the ability to see things from the grassroots level and know what is in people's minds.

Michael Portillo, 23 May 1995

◆

The fact is that Margaret Thatcher was never really a Conservative.

Robert Rhodes James, 15 July 1995

ACCORDING TO HER OPPONENTS

The papers are full of Margaret Thatcher. She has lent herself with grace and charm to every piece of photographer's gimmickry, and don't we all when the prize is big enough? What interests me now is how blooming she looks. She has never been prettier. I am interested because I understand this phenomenon. She may have been up late on the Finance Bill Committee, she's beset by enemies but she sails through it looking her best. I understand why – she's in love – in love with power, success and herself.

Barbara Castle's diary, 5 February 1975

◆

You know there are times, perhaps once every thirty years, when there is a sea-change in politics. It then does not matter what you say or what you do. There is a shift in what the public wants and what it approves of. I suspect there is now such a sea-change and it is for Mrs Thatcher.

James Callaghan, just prior to Mrs Thatcher's first general election victory, May 1979

◆

I can well understand the anxieties and pressures that must have been upon you during these weeks and I can understand that at this moment these pressures and these anxieties may be relieved, and I congratulate you.

Opposition leader Michael Foot following the retaking of the Falklands, June 1982

◆

Although we were not displeased in the Labour lady members' room when Margaret Thatcher got the Opposition leadership, we knew that she was what the American feminists irreverently call 'a man with tits' and would do little or nothing either for women in the House [of Commons] or women outside it.

Maureen Colquhoun MP

◆

To talk of Mrs Thatcher glorying in Falklands slaughter is to move the politics of the gutter to the politics of the abattoir.

David Owen, after Denis Healey had accused Mrs Thatcher of glorifying in slaughter, 2 June 1983

◆

If Margaret Thatcher wins on Thursday, I warn you not
to be ordinary, I warn you not to be young, I warn you
not to fall ill, and I warn you not to grow old.

Neil Kinnock, 7 June 1983

♦

She is the Castro of the western world – an embarrass-
ment to all her friends. All she lacks is the beard.

Denis Healey

♦

Some say Mrs Thatcher has a soft spot for the
Nottinghamshire miners. But she is like one of those
insects that consumes its mate after it has done the
business.

Frank Dobson

♦

Personally I think that she has the qualities of a very great
politician. I believe she has tremendous conviction, she
has drive, she has a commitment, she is totally genuine.

Michael Meacher, 1985

♦

Mrs Thatcher has a great sense of propriety and she
believes, as many women from her particular class believe,

and certainly women with important positions believe, that it's part of their duty to be solicitous and kindly in an official way, and she is fastidious in following that through.

Neil Kinnock, 1985

◆

She adds the diplomacy of Alf Garnett to the economics of Arthur Daley.

Denis Healey

◆

She believes she can treat TV interviewers just like her Cabinet.

Donald Anderson

◆

Ted Heath in drag.

Denis Healey

◆

I'm entirely in favour of Mrs Thatcher's visit to the Falklands. I find a bit of hesitation though, about her coming back.

John Mortimer

◆

She has fought resolutely for the class she represents and there are some lessons we might learn from that.

Tony Benn

◆

That appalling woman.

Neil Kinnock

◆

I cannot bring myself to vote for a woman who has been voice-trained to speak to me as though my dog has just died.

Keith Waterhouse

◆

We are definitely in for the last few weeks of Thatcherism, the last few weeks of that job-destroying, oil-wasting, truth-twisting, service-smashing, nation-splitting bunch of twisters under a one-person Government.

Neil Kinnock, May 1987

◆

She only went to Venice because somebody told her she could walk down the middle of the street.

Neil Kinnock on Mrs Thatcher's trip to the Venice economic summit during the general election campaign, 9 June 1987

◆

How do we know that next time, as always in the past, when President Reagan says jump, she will not reply 'How high?'

Denis Healey

◆

I have never considered Margaret Thatcher to be a Tory. In some senses she is a populist, she's an instinctive politician, she's not afraid of change, she's not afraid to challenge vested interests and doesn't mind if they are Tory interests – this is where she has an appeal. You cannot deny her political acumen and skills.

David Owen, May 1988

◆

When I hear the Prime Minister feeling sorry for the rest of the world, I understand why she has taken to calling herself 'we' – it's less lonely that way.

Neil Kinnock

◆

Mrs Thatcher will go down in history as one of the great Prime Ministers of this country.

Paddy Ashdown, 1988

◆

She is happier getting in and out of tanks than in and out of museums or theatre seats. She seems to derive more pleasure from admiring new missiles than great works of art. What else can we expect from an ex spam hoarder from Grantham, presiding over the social and economic decline of the country.

Tony Banks

◆

The Prime Minister tells us that she has given the French President a piece of her mind – not a gift I would receive with alacrity.

Denis Healey

◆

Trying to tell the Prime Minister anything is like making an important phone call and getting an answering machine.

David Steel

◆

She is about as environmentally friendly as the bubonic plague. I would be happy to see Margaret Thatcher stuffed, mounted, put in a glass case and left in a museum.

Tony Banks

◆

She is a heady mix of whisky and perfume.

David Owen

◆

Yesterday was hers, tomorrow is ours.

Neil Kinnock, on the tenth anniversary of her election, May 1989

◆

I'd rather kiss Mrs Thatcher.

Brian Clough, denying he was retiring, 25 October 1989

◆

It is now clear that the Prime Minister intends to become the Ceauşescu of the West and the main function of the Tory chairman at the next party conference will be to arrange sixty-nine standing ovations for her.

Denis Healey, November 1989

◆

I often compare the Prime Minister with Florence Nightingale. She stalks through the wards of our hospitals as a lady with a lamp – unfortunately it's a blowlamp.

Denis Healey

◆

I think she may need to put up a tough appearance to compensate for the fact she is not a man.

Andrew Faulds MP

◆

She believes in something. It is an old-fashioned idea.

Tony Benn

◆

The trouble is, she's like Maradona – always arguing with the referee.

David Owen, August 1990

◆

Papua New Guinea is the only other country with a poll tax. The time has come for the Tory Party to conclude that Mrs Thatcher could serve Great Britain best as our ambassador there.

Robin Cook, March 1990

◆

She is a half-mad old bag lady. The Finchley whinger. She said the poll tax was the Government's flagship. Like a captain she went down with her flagship. Unfortunately for the Conservative Party she keeps bobbing up again. Her head keeps appearing above the waves.

Tony Banks

◆

Mrs Thatcher likes to portray herself as Mother Earth. To the poor children of this country she is Mother Hubbard and her cupboard is always bare.

Joan Lestor, October 1990

◆

The problem for the Conservatives is that they were damned with Mrs Thatcher but are also damned without her.

Bryan Gould, 8 January 1991

◆

A lot of what Mrs Thatcher did I only blame her in part for. I blame [the Cabinet] for letting her get away with it.

Neil Kinnock, 11 May 1991

◆

You could fire a bazooka at her and inflict three large holes. Still she kept coming.

Roy Hattersley on her performance at Prime Minister's Question Time, October 1991

◆

When you hear that Mrs Thatcher is going to become Countess of Finchley, that certainly adds impetus to abolishing the House of Lords.

Charles Kennedy, October 1991

◆

I'm the sort of person Mrs Thatcher's parents warned her not to talk to as a little girl. I'm quite proud of that.

Ken Livingstone, 8 July 1995

ACCORDING TO FOREIGN LEADERS

She is trying to wear the trousers of Winston Churchill.

Leonid Brezhnev, 1979

◆

I couldn't be happier than I am over England's new Prime Minister... I've been rooting for her to become Prime Minister since our first meeting. If anyone can remind England of the greatness it knew during those dangerous days of World War II when alone and unafraid her people fought the Battle of Britain it will be the Prime Minister the English press has already nicknamed 'Maggie'.

Ronald Reagan, June 1979

◆

Somebody fix me a stiff drink. That's one hell of a tough lady.

General Alexander Haig after a meeting with Mrs Thatcher during the Falklands crisis, April 1982

◆

World affairs today demand the boldness and integrity of Churchill. In his absence, I know he would want us to look to you as the legendary Britannia, a special lady, the greatest defender of the realm.

President Reagan, September 1983

◆

The best man in Britain.

President Reagan, 1983

◆

On more than one occasion I said to him, Mr President, if you do that, Margaret Thatcher is going to be on the phone in an instant. And he said: 'Oh, I don't want that'.

Frank Carlucci on Ronald Reagan

◆

If I were married to her, I'd be sure and have the dinner on the table when she got home.

George Shultz, US Secretary of State 1982–89

◆

She has the eyes of Caligula, but the mouth of Marilyn
Monroe.

François Mitterrand, briefing his new Foreign Minister,
Roland Dumas

◆

As I prepare to depart this Office in January I take considerable satisfaction in knowing that Margaret Thatcher will
still reside at Number Ten Downing Street and will be there
to offer President Bush her friendship, cooperation and
advice. She's a world leader in every meaning of the word.

President Reagan, December 1988

◆

Mrs Thatcher, who can be so tough when she talks to her
European partners, is like a little girl of eight years old
when she talks to the President of the United States. You
have to cock your ear to hear her, she's really so touching.

François Mitterrand, 1989

◆

We know that God has endowed her with that great quality of not fidgeting when it is necessary to come to grips
with prickly nettles... Mrs Thatcher epitomises that
something extra in womanhood. Mrs Thatcher enhances
the meaning of womanhood.

Mangosuthu Buthelezi, October 1989

◆

The courage to state her case and side with the majority of black South Africans against a hostile and uninformed international community is the kind of courage which history only produces on rare occasions.

Mangosuthu Buthelezi, March 1990

◆

We don't all have the same warmongering ardour she is capable of at times.

Felipe González, August 1990

◆

Jesus, in Canada we erect a monument to a chap who loses three elections. In Britain you threaten to get rid of your Prime Minister when she wins three. What on earth is going on?

Brian Mulroney to Sir Bernard Ingham, 19 November 1990

◆

I liked her immediately. She was warm, feminine, gracious and intelligent, and it was evident from our first words that we were soul mates when it came to reducing Government and expanding economic freedom.

Ronald Reagan, 1990

◆

For us she is not the Iron Lady. She is the kind, dear Mrs Thatcher.

Alexander Dubček

◆

She pulled her notes out of her famous handbag. These were the prepared subjects for our talk. I got my folder full of notes, then the conversation began. And you know I felt that she was dropping those damned prepared topics. She put her notes in her handbag and pushed it away, and we simply began to talk, to argue, to discuss. I felt the same thing that she felt, that there was no hindrance to being able calmly to consider the most difficult questions.

Mikhail Gorbachev on their first meeting in 1984, BBC TV, 1993

◆

The difference between us is that I am living after Winston Churchill and she comes from the time before Winston Churchill.

Helmut Kohl, 16 October 1993

ACCORDING TO THE REST

A young woman of decided convictions.

Grantham Journal, July 1945

◆

[Mrs Thatcher] sounds as though she is always wearing a hat.

1970

◆

The most unpopular woman in Britain.

The Sun, 25 November 1971

◆

The Tories need more men like her.

Frank Johnson, *Daily Telegraph,* November 1974

◆

Mrs Thatcher's shadow Cabinet does credit to Mrs Thatcher herself. This shadow Cabinet is not notably to the right of the previous one. Indeed, if anything, it gives stronger positions of influence to the conservatism of compassion.

The Times, February 1975

◆

Margaret Thatcher's great strength seems to be the better people know her, the better they like her. But of course she has one great disadvantage. She is a daughter of the people and looks trim, as the daughters of the people desire to be.

Dame Rebecca West, *Sunday Times*, 25 July 1976

◆

I think that very few people on the *Sunday Times* were, by disposition or condition, pro her. We all thought she was a rather bossy, hand-baggy sort of lady. Already, that's the way we felt. But by the end of the lunch, she had argued so well, was so much in control of her facts, never lost her cool, and never let anybody get away with anything without pinning it down, and carried it off so well, that everyone around the table in their different ways was impressed.

Frank Giles, January 1990

◆

If she has a fault, it is being too tender-hearted.

Paul Johnson, 1977

♦

Perhaps I am a bit in love with Mrs Thatcher – platonically of course.

Woodrow Wyatt, 1977

♦

There is no side about her. She does not put on airs or assort herself. She is not aggressive or cocky. Nor is she like Barbara Castle who always seems to be trying to mark her personality on the occasion.

Sir Nicholas Henderson, December 1977

♦

Mrs Thatcher actually believes what she says and intends to act in a way consistent with her utterances if and when she becomes Prime Minister.

Ian Aitken, March 1978

♦

Don't be afraid to give her your advice. And don't be afraid to interrupt her or you'll never give that advice.

Sir Jack Rampton to Sir Bernard Ingham, September 1979

◆

She is the Enid Blyton of economics. Nothing must be allowed to spoil her simple plots.

Richard Holme, 10 September 1980

◆

Margaret Thatcher is now awesome. No longer just a national figure. She's inexorably turning into a bronze monument of herself. She is living out a legend in the Falklands which will go down in history.

Jean Rook, *Daily Express* columnist and 'First Lady of Fleet Street', 1983

◆

Hilda's Personal Photographer.

Slogan on T-shirts worn by photographers accompanying Mrs Thatcher on the final day of the 1983 election campaign

◆

Thatcherism is not an ideology, but a political style: a trick of presenting reasonable, rather pedestrian ideas in a way that drives reasonable men into a frothing rage.

Andrew Brown, *The Spectator*, 1984

◆

She's the only person I know who I don't think I've heard
say, 'I wonder whether'.

Sir William Pile, 1985

◆

Thatcher had just become Prime Minister; there was
talk whether it was an advance to have a woman Prime
Minister if it was someone with policies like hers: she
may be a woman but she isn't a sister. She may be a sister
but she isn't a comrade.

Caryl Churchill, 1987

◆

It may well be that economic Thatcherism [stressing the
importance of freedom and competition] would not be
indefinitely acceptable to the British public unless there
appeared to be a broader social dimension [stressing the
importance of responsibility and morality] as well.

Geoffrey Smith, *The Times*, 1988

◆

A few years ago, in an after-dinner speech, I cracked a
little joke about going to No. 10 and beginning my interview thus: 'Prime Minister, what is your answer to my
first question?' Among those who laughed loudest were
several members of Mrs Thatcher's Cabinet.

Sir Robin Day, 1989

◆

Nobody could have fought through the spoken and unspoken prejudice of the Fifties, the giggles and sneers of the Sixties, and the concealed male resentment and subtle male condescension of the Seventies and Eighties, without bearing the scars... An outsider to her party cannot know what she has to put up with.

Matthew Parris, *The Spectator*, 15 April 1989

◆

She has a pretty face, hasn't she? I expect she's pretty tough. Her great virtue is saying that two and two makes four, which is unpopular nowadays as it always has been. I adore Mrs Thatcher. At last politics make sense to me, which it hasn't since Stafford Cripps.

Philip Larkin

◆

One is, on the whole, glad that she is there, and we are here.

American columnist William Pfaff

◆

If I request that someone pass me the mustard, I do not get it until I have been told how obnoxious the Thatcher woman is. Hatred of Mrs Thatcher seems to have become obsessively implanted in the minds of the chattering classes and provides them with their principal source of conversation.

Brian Walden, 27 August 1989

◆

Mrs Thatcher gained power at a time when it seemed that the collective was depriving the individual of responsibility for his own life. Even crime was no longer an individual act: it was a response to social conditions [a view which insulted all decent people living in the same conditions but abstaining from criminal activity]. She disagreed... To dramatise this, she insisted 'society did not exist', though it was against an exaggerated view of society that she was reacting. Nothing she said would have been denied by Protestant churchmen before this century.

Allan Massie, *Sunday Times*, 1989

◆

Very like interviewing a telephone answering machine. You pose a question, you get an answer, and then you start to make a response and you find it's just going on and on and on.

Peter Jay on interviewing Margaret Thatcher

◆

The world shares our happiness – only Maggie continues to nag and scold.

Bild-Zeitung on German reunification, February 1990

◆

She's taken over from the Queen as someone who I dream about.

Kingsley Amis, *The Independent*, 25 March 1990

◆

One of the best-looking women I have ever met.

Kingsley Amis

◆

There is no one who is ever going to convince me that this is not a woman who is caring and compassionate and fiercely loyal to her friends.

Sir John Junor, 1990

◆

Came the 1960s and 1970s: corporatism, planning, protectionism and buttering up vested interest were tried by Conservative Governments as well as Labour, and failed. One or two Tories – Enoch Powell, Keith Joseph – began to look again at the laissez-faire tradition, and so did Margaret Thatcher. Of course, she has never been a true

Manchester liberal... Her own politics are rather those of Lord Copper and the Daily Beast, 'self-sufficiency at home, self-assertion abroad', and this combination of *enrichez-vous* and populist nationalism has made her in electoral terms the most successful party leader of the century.

Geoffrey Wheatcroft, *Encounter*, 1990

◆

Like interviewing the Niagara Falls – magnificent, unstoppable.

Ann Leslie, *Daily Mail*

◆

It is possible that she has accomplished what God sent her on Earth to do.

Mary Kenny, *Independent on Sunday*, 11 March 1990

◆

Both Margaret Thatcher and Keith Joseph had the courage of their convictions, but in a sense it was he who provided the convictions to match her courage.

Morrison Halcrow

◆

She was nice and cuddly.

Paul Gascoigne, following a Downing Street reception for the 1990 World Cup squad

◆

[She is] no puny leader, shaking a derisory fist as her enemies gather for the kill. Her self-image gives her a mighty stature, and she conveys this with every word of defiance she utters.

Hugo Young, *The Guardian*, 22 November 1990

◆

A man can forgive a woman anything except having greater reserves of testosterone than he does.

Wesley Pruden, *Washington Times*, 20 November 1990

◆

SHE'S TOO DAMN GOOD FOR THEM

Daily Mail headline, 23 November 1990

◆

The oddity about the Thatcher years is that the liberal influence has waxed rather than waned.

Lord Deedes, 21 September 1991

◆

Mrs Thatcher is not uncaring or cruel, but she is naive. She can't comprehend how absolutely useless, helpless and hopeless a good many people are, and is cursed with an incredible optimism and romanticism as to what the individual is capable of. If she kicks away the crutches, it's because she really does believe that everyone has the ability to walk without them.

Julie Burchill, 1992

◆

A big cat detained briefly in a poodle parlour, sharpening her claws on the velvet.

Matthew Parris on Lady Thatcher in the House of Lords, *Look Behind You!*, 1993

◆

You can't keep a good diva down.

Nancy Banks-Smith

◆

The Iron Lady wasn't perfect, critics of John Major are muttering, but at least she had lead in her pencil.

Rosalind Coward, *The Guardian*, 6 October 1993

◆

It helps if Mrs Thatcher, as she proceeds with her unassailable argument, progresses physically further and further across the sofa until she is practically upon the interviewer.

Terry Coleman on interviewing Margaret Thatcher, *The Guardian*, 6 November 1993

◆

Those of us who write about these things should admit that Margaret Thatcher's *The Downing Street Years* was a far better book than we expected. It reads well and is often gripping. It is one-sided, self-confident, insincere, single-minded, selective, deeply unfair and rather magnificent – like its author. The book's authenticity may be questioned but the unwitting picture of her will endure.

Stephen Spender, *Sunday Telegraph*, 12 December 1993

◆

You don't look too bad at all.

John Humphrys just before interviewing her, 11 July 1995

◆

I was in love with her, yes, but I suppose in the best platonic manner, because, well, she was a marvellous girl. At that time, well, she still can – she looked rather beautiful. But her skin was glowing and she had very fine legs.

Woodrow Wyatt, *Independent on Sunday*, November 1996

◆

We are true Thatcherites. She was the first Spice Girl, the
pioneer of our ideology, girl power. What matters in life
is the ability to rise and do anything... I like the woman.
Even if her policies were hard-headed. Socialism is bad.

Geri Halliwell of the Spice Girls, *The Sun*, 13 December 1996

◆

Mrs Thatcher used to be like one of the lions in Trafalgar
Square. Malcolm Rifkind is like one of the pigeons.

Dr Alan Sked, leader of the UK Independence Party, 16
December 1996

YES, PRIME MINISTER

The following is the text of a Yes, Prime Minister *sketch written and conceived by Margaret Thatcher's Press Secretary, Sir Bernard Ingham. The text was refined in consultation with the Prime Minister and her staff. It was performed by Margaret Thatcher, Paul Eddington (Jim Hacker) and Nigel Hawthorne (Sir Humphrey Appleby) in January 1984.*

◆

Margaret Thatcher: Good morning Jim, Sir Humphrey. Do come in and sit down. How's your wife? Is she well?

Jim Hacker: [puzzled] Oh yes, fine Prime Minister, fine I thank you. Yes, fine.

MT: Good. So pleased. I've been meaning to have a word with you for some time. I've got an idea.

JH: [brightening visibly] An idea, Prime Minister? Oh good!

Sir Humphrey: [guardedly] An idea, Prime Minister?

MT: Well, not really an idea. I've done quite a bit of thinking, and I'm sure you, Jim, are quite the man to carry it out. It's got to do with a kind of institution and you are responsible for institutions aren't you?

Sir H: [cautiously] Institutions, Prime Minister?

JH: [decisively] Oh yes, institutions fall to me. Most definitely. And you want me to set one up, I suppose.

MT: Set one up? Certainly not, I want you to get rid of one.

JH: [astonished] Get rid of one, Prime Minister?

MT: Yes, it's all very simple. I want you to abolish economists.

JH: [mouth open] Abolish economists, Prime Minister?

MT: Yes, abolish economists – quickly.

Sir H: [silkily] All of them, Prime Minister?

MT: Yes, all of them. They never agree on anything. They just fill the heads of politicians with all sorts of curious notions, like the more you spend, the richer you get.

JH: [coming round to the idea] I take your point, Prime Minister. Can't have the nation's time wasted on curious notions, can we? No.

Sir H: [sternly] Minister!

MT: Quite right Jim. Absolute waste of time. Simply got to go.

JH: [uncertain] Simply got to go.

MT: [motherly] Yes, Jim. Don't worry. If it all goes wrong I shall get the blame. But if it goes right – as it will – then you'll get the credit for redeploying a lot of misapplied resources. Probably get promotion too.

Sir H: [indignantly] Resources? Resources, Prime Minister? Surely we're talking about economists.

MT: Were, Sir Humphrey. Were.

JH: [decisively] Yes, Humphrey, were. We're going to get rid of them.

MT: Well, it's all settled then. I'll look forward to receiving your plan for abolition soon. Tomorrow, shall we say? I'd like you to announce it before it all leaks.

JH: [brightly] Tomorrow then, Prime Minister?

MT: Yes, well sort it out. Now, Sir Humphrey – what did you say your degree was?

Sir H: [innocently] Degree, Prime Minister?

MT: [firmly] Yes, Sir Humphrey, degree. Your degree. You have one, I take it – most permanent secretaries do – or perhaps two.

Sir H: [modestly] Er. Well actually, Prime Minister, a double first.

MT: Congratulations, Sir Humphrey, but what's it in?

Sir H: [weakly] Politics – er ... and, er ... economics.

MT: [soothingly] Capital, my dear Sir Humphrey. You'll know exactly where to start.

Sir H: [bleakly] Yes, Prime Minister.

◆

STICKS AND STONES

During her political career, Margaret Thatcher was probably called more names and given more nicknames than any other living politician. What follows is but a small selection...

Attila the Hen from No. 10 – Arthur Scargill

Bargain Basement Boudicca – Denis Healey

Baroness Belgrano – Edward Pearce

Boss – *Private Eye*

Catherine the Great of Finchley – Denis Healey

David Owen in drag – *Rhodesia Herald*

Egotistical Flea in a Fit – Neil Kinnock

Great She Elephant – Denis Healey

Grocer's Daughter – Valéry Giscard D'Estaing

Heather – *Private Eye*

High Taxer Thatcher – Neil Kinnock

Iron Lady – *Red Star* newspaper (Moscow)

Iron Maiden – Marjorie Proops

La Passionara of Privilege – Denis Healey

Lady Macbeth – Roy Hattersley

Maggots Scratcher – Steven Berkoff

Man with Tits – Maureen Colquhoun

Mother – Tory MPs

Nanny of the Nation – Germaine Greer

Old Iron Knickers – Ron Brown

Parrot on Ronald Reagan's Shoulder – Denis Healey

Pétain in Petticoats – Denis Healey

Plutonium Blonde – Arthur Scargill

President Reagan's Glove Puppet – Gerald Kaufman

Rambina – Chris Buckland

Ramobona – Denis Healey

Rhoda the Rhino – Denis Healey

Surrogate Man – Glenys Kinnock

That Bloody Woman – Dennis Canavan

Thatch – Ben Elton

Thatcher Milk Snatcher – *The Sun*

Thatchertollah – Neil Kinnock

The Blessed Margaret – Norman St John-Stevas

The Immaculate Misconception – Norman St John-Stevas

Thieving Magpie – Gerald Kaufman

TINA (There Is No Alternative) – *Private Eye*

Westminster Ripper – Dennis Skinner

Wicked Witch of the West – Gerald Kaufman

Winston Churchill in Drag – Denis Healey

APPENDIX

MAGGIE'S MINISTERS

In her eleven and a half years in power, sixty Ministers served in Mrs Thatcher's Cabinet – of them, only one was a woman.

Humphrey Atkins 1979–82 Resigned (Falklands)
Kenneth Baker 1985–90 Final Cabinet
Lord Belstead 1987–90 Final Cabinet
John Biffen 1979–87 Sacked
Leon Brittan 1981–86 Resigned (Westland)
Peter Brooke 1987–90 Final Cabinet
Mark Carlisle 1979–81 Sacked
Lord Carrington 1979–82 Resigned (Falklands)
Paul Channon 1986–89 Sacked
Kenneth Clarke 1985–90 Final Cabinet
Lord Cockfield 1982–84 Sacked
Nicholas Edwards 1979–87 Sacked
Norman Fowler 1981–90 Resigned (Personal reasons)
Sir Ian Gilmour 1979–81 Sacked

Earl of Gowrie 1984–85 Resigned (Financial reasons)

John Gummer 1989–90 Final Cabinet

Lord Hailsham 1979–87 Sacked

Sir Michael Havers 1979–87 Sacked

Michael Heseltine 1979–86 Resigned (Westland)

Michael Howard 1990 Final Cabinet

Sir Geoffrey Howe 1979–90 Resigned (Europe)

David Howell 1979–81 Sacked

David Hunt 1990 Final Cabinet

Douglas Hurd 1984–90 Final Cabinet

Patrick Jenkin 1979–85 Sacked

Michael Jopling 1979–87 Sacked

Sir Keith Joseph 1979–86 Resigned (Personal reasons)

Tom King 1983–90 Final Cabinet

Norman Lamont 1989–90 Final Cabinet

Nigel Lawson 1981–89 Resigned (Economic policy)

Peter Lilley 1990 Final Cabinet

John MacGregor 1985–90 Final Cabinet

Lord Mackay of Clashfern 1987–90 Final Cabinet

John Major 1987–90 Final Cabinet

Angus Maude 1979–81 Sacked

Sir Patrick Mayhew 1987–90 Final Cabinet

John Moore 1986–89 Sacked

Tony Newton 1988–90 Final Cabinet

Sir John Nott 1979–83 Resigned (Personal reasons)

Cecil Parkinson 1979–83, 87–90 Final Cabinet

Christopher Patten 1989–90 Final Cabinet

James Prior 1979–84 Sacked

Francis Pym 1979–83 Sacked

Peter Rees 1983–85 Sacked

Tim Renton 1989–90 Final Cabinet

Nicholas Ridley 1981–90 Resigned (Anti-German comments)

Malcolm Rifkind 1986–90 Final Cabinet

Norman St John-Stevas 1979–81 Sacked

Lord Soames 1979–81 Sacked

Norman Tebbit 1981–87 Resigned (Personal reasons)

David Waddington 1987–90 Final Cabinet

John Wakeham 1983–90 Final Cabinet

William Waldegrave 1990 Final Cabinet

Peter Walker 1979–90 Resigned (Personal reasons)

William Whitelaw 1979–88 Resigned (Health)

Lady Young 1982–83 Sacked

Lord Young 1984–89 Resigned (Personal reasons)

George Younger 1979–89 Resigned (Personal reasons)

CAREER CHRONOLOGY

13 October 1925 – Born in Grantham.

23 February 1950 – Fights Dartford constituency at general election.

25 October 1951 – Fights Dartford constituency at general election.

8 October 1959 – Wins Finchley constituency at general election.

5 February 1960 – Makes maiden speech in the House of Commons.

February–October 1960 – Parliamentary passage of MT's Public Bodies (Admission of the Press to Meetings) Bill.

9 October 1961 – Appointed Parliamentary Secretary at the Ministry for Pensions and National Insurance in Harold Macmillan's Government.

28 October 1964 – Appointed Opposition Spokesman on Pensions.

5 October 1965 – Appointed shadow Spokesman for Housing and Land.

19 April 1966 – Appointed shadow Treasury Spokesman under Iain Macleod.

12 October 1966 – Makes first speech from the platform at the Conservative Party Conference.

10 October 1967 – Appointed to the shadow Cabinet as shadow Spokesman on Fuel and Power.

10 October 1968 – Gives annual Conservative Political Centre lecture on 'What's wrong with politics'.

14 November 1968 – Appointed shadow Transport Spokesman.

21 November 1969 – Appointed shadow Education Spokesman.

19 June 1970 – Appointed Secretary of State for Education in Edward Heath's Cabinet.

May 1974 – Forms Centre for Policy Studies think tank with Sir Keith Joseph.

4 February 1975 – Defeats Edward Heath in first round of Conservative Party leadership election.

11 February 1975 – Elected leader of the Conservative Party.

28 March 1979 – Labour Government is defeated on a motion of no confidence.

3 May 1979 – Leads Conservative Party to general election victory with a majority of forty-three.

12 June 1979 – Budget cuts standard rate of income tax from 33p to 30p but VAT is nearly doubled to 15 per cent.

5 May 1980 – Orders SAS to storm Iranian embassy after terrorist siege.

5 January 1981 – First reshuffle involved the sacking of Norman St John-Stevas.

1 March 1981 – Refuses to bow to IRA hunger striker's demands for political status.

14 September 1981 – Second Cabinet reshuffle sees sacking of Ian Gilmour and Christopher Soames and promotion of Nigel Lawson, Cecil Parkinson and Norman Tebbit. Jim Prior moved to Northern Ireland from Employment.

2 April 1982 – Argentina invades the Falklands.

2 May 1982 – Gives Task Force permission to sink Argentinean battle cruiser *General Belgrano*.

14 June 1982 – British forces capture Port Stanley ending the Falklands War.

9 June 1983 – Leads Conservative Party to a second general election victory with a record majority of 144.

11 June 1983 – Reshuffles Cabinet. Nigel Lawson becomes Chancellor, Leon Brittan becomes Home Secretary and Sir Geoffrey Howe goes to the Foreign Office.

25 October 1983 – Condemns US invasion of Grenada.

22 April 1984 – Breaks off diplomatic relations with Libya over shooting of WPC Yvonne Fletcher outside the Libyan Embassy.

12 October 1984 – IRA bomb explodes at the Grand Hotel in Brighton yards from Margaret Thatcher's room.

15 December 1984 – First meeting with Mikhail Gorbachev at Chequers.

19 December 1984 – Signs agreement with China transferring Hong Kong to China in 1997.

20 February 1985 – Addresses both Houses of the US Congress.

3 March 1985 – National Union of Mineworkers calls off year long coal strike.

5 September 1985 – Cabinet reshuffle sees Douglas Hurd, John MacGregor, Kenneth Clarke and Kenneth Baker join the Cabinet.

15 November 1985 – Signs Anglo-Irish Agreement.

9 January 1986 – Defence Secretary Michael Heseltine resigns from the Cabinet over the Westland Affair.

17 February 1986 – Signs the Single European Act.

15 April 1986 – Allows US bombers to fly from Britain to bomb Libyan targets.

11 June 1987 – Leads Conservative Party to a third general election victory with a majority of 101.

15 March 1988 – Budget cuts basic rate of tax to 25p and the top rate to 40p.

20 September 1988 – Makes controversial speech in Bruges.

26 June 1989 – Nigel Lawson and Sir Geoffrey Howe secretly threaten to resign if MT does not agree to their policy on joining the Exchange Rate Mechanism.

24 July 1989 – Cabinet reshuffle demotes Sir Geoffrey Howe. John Major becomes Foreign Secretary.

26 October 1989 – Nigel Lawson resigns as Chancellor. John Major takes over.

5 December 1989 – Wins Conservative Party leadership contest by 314 to Sir Anthony Meyer's 33 votes with 27 abstentions.

14 July 1990 – Key Cabinet ally Nicholas Ridley resigns following anti-German comments.

30 July 1990 – Another ally, former PPS Ian Gow, is killed by an IRA car bomb.

2 August 1990 – Iraq invades Kuwait. MT is with George Bush at Aspen.

3 October 1990 – Bows to pressure from Chancellor John Major to enter the ERM.

27 October 1990 – Special EC summit in Rome prompts 'No, No, No' to a single currency.

1 November 1990 – Sir Geoffrey Howe resigns from the Cabinet.

22 November 1990 – Resignation as Conservative Party leader.

28 November 1990 – Last day as Prime Minister.

June 1991 – Announces she will stand down as an MP at the next general election.

9 April 1992 – Stands down as Member of Parliament for Finchley.

30 June 1992 – Takes her seat in the House of Lords as Baroness Thatcher of Kesteven.

2 July 1992 – Makes her maiden speech in the House of Lords.

October 1993 – First volume of memoirs, *The Downing Street Years*, is published.

22 April 1995 – Appointed to the Order of the Garter, the UK's highest order of chivalry.

October 1995 – Second volume of memoirs, *The Path to Power*, is published.

June 1997 – Endorses William Hague for the Conservative Party leadership race.

October 1999 – Gives her first speech to a Conservative Party Conference in nine years.

June 2001 – Supports Iain Duncan Smith for Conservative Party leader.

March 2002 – Publishes her third book, *Statecraft: Strategies for a Changing World.*

26 June 2003 – Widowed when her husband, Denis Thatcher, passes away.

11 June 2004 – Delivers a eulogy via videotape at Ronald Reagan's funeral.

13 October 2005 – Celebrates her eightieth birthday, among the Royal Family and the Prime Minister.

February 2007 – Becomes the first Prime Minister of the UK to be honoured with a statue in the Houses of Parliament while still living.

AFTERWORD

If someone had told me a few years ago that I would edit a book on Margaret Thatcher, I'd have thought they were mad. Thatcher had been out of office for two years by the time I was born, and the idea that a young boy from a working-class area in Newport, South Wales, would become the staunchest of Thatcherites could best be described as 'highly unlikely'. Though my parents were careful never to push me into taking certain views, we were clearly a Labour-supporting family, and that meant Thatcher was a dirty word.

Ironically, it was my family's encouragement to be well-read in history and current affairs that led me to study and believe in Thatcher's vision. Andrew Marr's wonderful *A History of Modern Britain* was the trigger. As I watched the episode on Margaret Thatcher and the 1980s, I increasingly found myself thinking 'I agree with this woman' and I wanted to discover more about her. Weeks later, I collected the *Daily Telegraph*'s DVD series on her time in office and, by the time I had watched them all, I was a committed Thatcherite. I saved up my paper round money to buy as many books on Thatcher as I could get my hands on. So inspired by her example, I set up a branch of Conservative Future in my home city, and went on to become Chairman of Conservative Future Wales. Being a Thatcherite in South Wales can, of course, be a lonely existence. But the battle of ideas and the opportunity to argue and debate Thatcherite-Conservative principles (as my long-suffering teachers and family will attest), is still so important.

Margaret Thatcher's legacy still has an important and telling influence on British political life, in the same way that Gladstone and Disraeli did a century earlier. Even though she hasn't made a full speech for ten years, she retains the ability to make news and influence current-day politicians in a way no other politician can. No other Prime Minister can say they have had a Hollywood block-buster made about their time in office while they have been alive. The reaction to that film shows that she is still loved and hated in equal measures. The bile and venom on the internet whenever her name is mentioned has to be seen to be believed. She is often held to be responsible for all the ills of today's economy – including the recent banking crisis – and society, even though it is two decades since she left Downing Street.

For those of us who remain firm adherents and defenders of the legacy of her Governments, we relish the opportunity to fight back. We point out how much of a basket case the British economy was in 1979, when Thatcher won her first election as Conservative leader. Only three years earlier the Labour Chancellor, Denis

Healey, had humiliatingly been forced to go to the IMF. Nationalised industries were overmanned and inefficient and British industry was clinging on to the glories of an industrial past, without realising that other countries were overtaking us in an increasingly competitive international market. Thatcher took on the weak management and rampant trade unions which had combined to prevent the modernisation of working practices, devastating the British car, steel and coal industries. She forced industrial leaders to wake up to the fact that without standing up to the trade unions they might as well give up. But Thatcher's achievements were much more significant than the economic recovery alone. She woke up a nation which had seemed accustomed to a declining influence in world affairs, post-Suez. It wasn't just the Falklands War that put the Great back into Great Britain; it was the strong diplomacy deployed in her dealings with the European Community and the Soviet bloc that restored a pride and self respect that had been missing for decades.

Margaret Thatcher was able to lead, to inspire, to motivate in a way few politicians in this country have been able to emulate since. Though times have changed since the 1980s, and specific policies used then might not be the medicine required today, the principles that underpinned Thatcher's legacy are as true now as they were thirty years ago.

I am therefore immensely proud to have compiled this book. I have tried to include all of Thatcher's well-known remarks, as well as some more obscure ones. It is safe to say that this book dispels the myth that Margaret

Thatcher didn't have a sense of humour. I do hope reading this book provided the same entertainment, information and inspiration that compiling it did for me.

Despite my grandparents' protests, they are examples of why Thatcher's Britain worked. Thanks to her, one set bought their council house and strived to own their own business, enabling my grandad to finally leave his manual labour job, while the other set owned and ran three pubs in Newport during the 1980s – businesses which I know gave my grandfather some of the most rewarding times of his life. I will always be grateful to my family – they have always encouraged me to care about politics and to stand up for what I believe. This year I finally convinced my father to join the Conservative Party and he even stood for election as a councillor. Though unsuccessful, watching my mum and dad engage in local politics and campaigning made me a very proud son.

As one of Lady Thatcher's closest friends, Conor Burns, Member of Parliament for Bournemouth West, is always quick to remind people of the words of wisdom that Margaret Thatcher espoused. His treasure trove of Thatcher anecdotes will keep me entertained for a lifetime and I thank him for his help compiling this book.

I am equally grateful to Chris Collins whose work for the Margaret Thatcher Foundation is beyond compare. The MargaretThatcher.org website is a tremendous source of Thatcher wisdom. I highly recommend it.

I would like to thank the individuals who have made me feel proud to be part of the Conservative movement and who will continue the Thatcher legacy for decades to come. In particular, Simon Richards of The Freedom Association, Donal Blaney of the Young Britons' Foundation, Ryan Bourne of the Centre for Policy Studies, Mark Littlewood of the Institute of Economic Affairs, Matthew Elliott of the TaxPayers' Alliance, and Madsen Pirie of the Adam Smith Institute.

Last but not least, I will be eternally grateful to Iain Dale, who took a punt by hiring this ballsy young Welshman as his assistant. Two years on I am still learning from him, it is amazing to say that he is my boss and I am still enjoying it as much as I ever have.

Grant Tucker
London, July 2012

SELECT READING

Abse, Leo, *Margaret Daughter of Beatrice* (Jonathan Cape, 1989)

Arnold, Bruce, *Margaret Thatcher: A Study in Power* (Hamish Hamilton, 1984)

Baker, Kenneth, *The Turbulent Years – My Life in Politics* (Faber and Faber, 1993)

Berlinski, Claire, *There is No Alternative: Why Margaret Thatcher Matters* (Basic Books, 2008)

Campbell, John, *Margaret Thatcher Volume One – The Grocer's Daughter* (Vintage, 2007)

Campbell, John, *Margaret Thatcher Volume Two – The Iron Lady* (Vintage, 2007)

Clark, Alan, *Diaries* (Weidenfeld and Nicolson, 1994)

Collins, Ian, *Westminster Exposed* (Jarrold, 1988)

Cosgrave, Patrick, *Margaret Thatcher: A Tory and Her Party* (Hutchinson, 1978)

Cosgrave, Patrick, *Thatcher: The First Term* (Bodley Head, 1985)

Dale, Iain, *Memories of Maggie: A Portrait of Margaret Thatcher* (Politico's Publishing, 2000)

Dale, Iain, *Margaret Thatcher: A Tribute in Pictures and Words* (Weidenfeld and Nicolson, 2005)

Dale, Iain, *Margaret Thatcher: In Her Own Words* (Biteback, 2010)

Day, Sir Robin, *Grand Inquisitor* (Weidenfeld and Nicolson, 1989)

Freedman, Sir Lawrence, *The Official History of the Falklands Campaign* (Routledge, 2007)

Gardiner MP, George, *Margaret Thatcher* (William Kimber, 1975)

Gove, Michael, *Michael Portillo – Future of the Right* (Fourth Estate, 1995)

Green, Jonathon, *Book of Political Quotes* (Angus and Robertson, 1982)

Harris, Kenneth, *Thatcher* (Weidenfeld and Nicolson, 1988)

Harris, Robert, *Good and Faithful Servant* (Faber and Faber, 1990)

Hawke, Bob, *The Hawke Memoirs* (Heinemann, 1994)

Henderson, Sir Nicholas, *Mandarin* (Weidenfeld and Nicolson, 1994)

Henning, Chuck, *Wit and Wisdom of Politics* (Fulcrum, 1992)

Howe, Sir Geoffrey, *Conflict of Loyalty* (Macmillan, 1994)

Ingham, Bernard, *Kill the Messenger* (HarperCollins, 1993)

Jarman, Colin, *Guinness Dictionary of Poisonous Quotes* (Guinness, 1991)

Jenkins, Roy, *A Life at the Centre* (Macmillan, 1991)

Jenkins, Simon, *Thatcher and Sons: A Revolution in Three Acts* (Penguin, 2007)

Jones, Graham, *Forked Tongues* (Century, 1984)

Jones, Graham, *Forked Tongues Annual* (Century, 1985)

Jones, Graham, *Official Candidate's Book of Political Insults* (Century, 1987)

Junor, Sir John, *Listening for a Midnight Tram* (Chapmans, 1990)

Junor, Penny, *Margaret Thatcher: Wife, Mother, Politician* (Sidgwick and Jackson, 1983)

Knight, Greg, *Honourable Insults* (Robson Books, 1990)

Knight, Greg, *Parliamentary Sauce* (Robson Books, 1993)

Lawson, Nigel, *The View from Number 11* (Bantam, 1992)

Lewis, Russell, *Margaret Thatcher, A Personal and Political Biography – Updated* (Routledge, 1983)

McFadyean, Melanie, *Thatcher's Reign – A Bad Case of the Blues* (Chatto and Windus, 1984)

Mayer, Allan, *Madam Prime Minister* (Newsweek Books (US), 1979)

Millar, Ronald, *A View from the Wings* (Weidenfeld and Nicolson, 1993)

Money, Ernle, *Margaret Thatcher: First Lady of the House* (Leslie Frewin, 1975)

Murray, Patricia, *Margaret Thatcher: A Profile* (W.H. Allen, 1978)

Ogden, Chris, *Maggie: An Intimate Portrait of a Woman in Power* (Simon and Schuster (US), 1992)

Parkinson, Cecil, *Right at the Centre* (Weidenfeld and Nicolson, 1992)

Parris, Matthew and Mason, Phil, *Read My Lips* (Robson Books, 1996)

Prior, James, *Balance of Power* (Hamish Hamilton, 1986)

Ranelagh, John, *Thatcher's People* (HarperCollins, 1991)

Ridley, Nicholas, *My Style of Government* (Century, 1991)

Rogers, Michael, *Political Quotes* (Sphere, 1982)

Sharp, Paul, *Thatcher's Diplomacy: The Revival of British Foreign Policy* (Palgrave Macmillan, 1999)

Smith, Geoffrey, *Reagan and Thatcher* (Bodley Head, 1990)

Thatcher, Carol, *Diary of an Election* (Sidgwick and Jackson, 1983)

Thatcher, Carol, *Below the Parapet* (HarperCollins, 1996)

Thatcher, Carol, *A Swim-on Part in the Goldfish Bowl* (Headline Review, 2008)

Thatcher, Margaret, *Speeches to the Conservative Party Conference 1975–88* (CPC, 1989)

Thatcher, Margaret, *The Downing Street Years* (HarperCollins, 1993)

Thatcher, Margaret, *The Path to Power* (HarperCollins, 1995)

Thatcher, Margaret, *Statecraft: Strategies for a Changing World* (HarperCollins, 2002)

Thompson, Andrew, *Margaret Thatcher: The Woman Within* (W.H. Allen, 1989)

Tomlinson, Gerald, *Speaker's Treasury of Political Stories, Anecdotes and Humour* (MJF, 1990)

Urban, George, *Diplomacy and Disillusion* (I. B. Tauris, 1996)

Wapshott, Nicholas and Brock, George, *Thatcher* (Macdonald, 1983)

Wapshott, Nicholas, *Ronald Reagan and Margaret Thatcher: A Political Marriage* (Sentinel, 2007)

Watkins, Alan, *A Conservative Coup* (Duckworth, 1991)

Young, Hugo, *The Thatcher Phenomenon* (BBC Books, 1985)

Young, Hugo, *One of Us* (Macmillan, 1989)

Also available from Biteback

Prime Minister Boris
and other things that never happened

Iain Dale and Duncan Brack

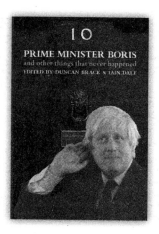

The grand passage of political history is steered by a combination of events great and small; assessing how matters might have turned out under different circumstances is one of the most intriguing – and entertaining – historical exercises. This book imagines such tantalising political questions as: What if Nixon had beaten JFK in 1960? What if Arnold Schwarznegger had been able to run for President? And, of course, what if Boris Johnson were to become Prime Minister in 2016?

384pp paperback, £9.99
Available now from all good bookshops or order from
www.bitebackpublishing.com

Also available from Biteback

Margaret Thatcher In Her Own Words (CD)

Edited by Iain Dale

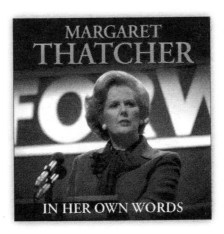

Margaret Thatcher was Britain's longest serving twentieth-century Prime Minister. She towered over the British political landscape for more than a decade, and transformed the face of Britain. Biteback Publishing is proud to release this unique collection of Margaret Thatcher's greatest and most famous utterances.

The 3 CDs contain 56 clips including: Where there is Discord • The Lady's Not for Turning • Falklands War Speeches • Bruges Speech • No! No! No! • I'm Enjoying This!

CD, £19.99
Available now from all good bookshops
www.bitebackpublishing.com